# *Dreamers of Dreams*

**Malcolm Young**

Solomon
Press

Published by Solomon Press
Unit 1, Rydon Farm, West Newton
Somerset, TA7 0BZ
Tel: 01278 661 300
Email: info@solomon-press.com

Web site: www.solomon-press.com


© Malcolm Young 2001
First published 2001


ISBN 1 901724 220

Design and typesetting by Pedeke Ltd, Bridgwater, Somerset
Printed in Great Britain by Stephens and George, Merthyr Tydfil, Wales

For

Xavier and Tuppence

# CONTENTS

We are the music-makers,
        And we are the dreamers of dreams,
Wandering by lone sea-breakers,
        And sitting by desolate streams;
World losers and world forsakers,
        On whom the pale moon gleams:
Yet we are the movers and shakers
        Of the world for ever, it seems.

With wonderful deathless ditties
        We build up the world's great cities,
And out of a fabulous story
        We fashion an empire's glory:
One man with a dream, at pleasure,
        Shall go forth and conquer a crown;
And three with a new song's measure
        Can trample an empire down.

We, in the ages lying
        In the buried past of the earth,
Built Nineveh with our sighing,
        And Babel itself with our mirth;
And o'erthrew them with prophesying
        To the old of the new world's worth;
For each age is a dream that is dying,
        Or one that is coming to birth.


A. W. E. O'Shaughnessy

# INTRODUCTION

Poets are the music-makers; they are the dreamers of dreams, the storytellers; through their verses we can be transported into the past, the future, anywhere in this world, or out of it; through their eyes we can see something of the meaning of life, and we can see ourselves.

In selecting poems to include in this book I have tried to cover as many areas as possible - songs and ballads, the stories of narrative poems, the more formal verse forms of sonnets, odes and elegies, as well as a wide range of subjects from the serious to the light-hearted.

For my source I have drawn mainly on the great poets of the past because I believe that they still have a great deal to offer to young people today. That enormous body of poems produced over the past three or four hundred years forms part of our cultural heritage and through the eyes of the great poets of the past we can see people and places and events that might otherwise be lost to us. The poems are still wonderfully entertaining to read although there is a danger that the diminishing vocabulary of the latter part of the twentieth century might lead some to dismiss some of the older works in impatience, when just a little thought and perseverance would enable them to enjoy them fully.

Apart from all that, studying the poems reproduced here will, I hope, familiarise the new student of poetry with the many and varied forms that verse can take. I would like to think that after reading this book you will know something more about rhythm and metre, rhyme and form, and the many devices that poets employ, but above all that you will appreciate what an extremely disciplined kind of writing poetry is.

It is good if you want to write down your thoughts, and express your ideas and views on life and this exciting world we live in; but if you want to write these things as poetry, you really should learn the disciplines that will enable you to produce something that is ultimately far more satisfying.

I hope that you will enjoy reading the poems I have selected, as much as some of them have been enjoyed by generations past, and I hope that some of you will become the poets of the Twenty-first Century.

On the following pages you will find some notes on Rhythm, Metre and Rhyme, to help you to understand these very basic ingredients of poetry.

**Rhythm in poetry** is the more-or-less regular beat that is created by the way in which the sounds of words is arranged.

**Metre** is what we call our way of measuring the pattern of sounds that we create.

To explore Rhythm and Metre fully, it is important to be quite clear about syllables.

**A syllable** is a single sound of language.

Words of one syllable make one sound.
　　　　　　　Examples:  *bee, cat, shop, ear, up.*

Words of two syllables make two sounds.
　　　　　　　Examples:  *paper, window, receive, perfect, defend.*

And so on ...
Three syllables:　　　　*miserly, liberty, fantastic, defensive, computer.*

Four:　　　　　　　*Victorian, considerate, anonymous, interruption, separation.*

Five:　　　　　　　*interpretation, Elizabethan, astronomical, disintegration.*

Six:　　　　　　　*uncoordinated, differentiation, intercontinental, misinterpretation.*

*Now it's your turn to prove that you really are at ease with syllables.*

**Try this exercise:**  Time allowed:  10 minutes.  No dictionaries.

Write six lists of four words, similar to those above, with 1, 2, 3, 4, 5 and 6 syllables.

Scoring:  1 mark for each syllable.

How did you do?

30+ Fair;  45+ Good;  60+ Very Good;  70+ Excellent;  maximum score 84  Genius!

The rhythm in a line of verse depends to a large extent on the arrangement of **stressed** and **unstressed** syllables. These are also called **accented** and **unaccented** syllables.

Look at these words of two syllables:
   **PAper, WINdow, SWEEping, TROUble.**
Notice that they all have the same pattern with the **stress** or **accent** on the first syllable.

Now look at these words:
   **inTEND, deCEIVE, comPLETE, beHIND**
Notice that these words all have the **stress** or **accent** on the second syllable.

In discussing the metre of poetry certain marks are used to show a stressed syllable ( ′ )
and an unstressed syllable ( ˘ )
Therefore the words used as examples above may be marked:

   **páper, wíndow, swéeping   -   inténd, decéive, compléte**

Now look at these words of three syllables and note where the stressed syllable is:

   **interrúpt, puppeteér, entertáin, cigare′tte**

   **mérrily, wándering, mínister, réadiness**

   **distúrbance, reáction, umbrélla, extínguish**

For those who like to know the correct names for such things:

   **iamb:**   an unstressed syllable followed by a stressed syllable

   **trochee:**   a stressed syllable followed by an unstressed

   **anapest:**   two unstressed syllables followed by a stressed syllable

   **dactyl:**   one stressed syllable followed by two unstressed syllables

**Foot** is the word we use to describe a metrical unit, made up of one stressed and one or more unstressed syllables.

Now you can look at lines of verse and describe **how they are constructed**.

This is the first line of William Wordsworth's famous poem 'Daffodils':

*I wandered lonely as a cloud*

It is made up of four feet:   **I wan / dered lone / ly as / a cloud**

Each of those feet is an iamb (see above) :  **Ĭ wán / dĕred lóne / lў ás / ă clóud**

Now notice how the second line follows exactly the same pattern:

**Thăt flóats / ŏn hígh / o'er váles / ănd hílls**

The next three lines continue the rhythm:

*When all at once I saw a crowd,*
*A host of golden daffodils;*
*Beside the lake, beneath the trees,*

Only in the final line of the verse does the rhythm change slightly:

**flútt erĭng / ănd dánc / ĭng ín / thĕ bréeze.**

Can you see that the first foot is a trochee?

Now read the second verse aloud and notice that it follows exactly the same pattern as the first verse.

*Continuous as the stars that shine*
*And twinkle in the milky way,*
*They stretched in never-ending line*
*Along the margin of a bay:*
*Ten thousand saw I at a glance,*
*Tossing their heads in sprightly dance.*

There are two more verses to this poem, which you may like to read on page 77.

You may also wish to know that lines of verse are given names according to the number of feet they contain.

one foot:  **monometer**        two feet:  **dimeter**
three feet: **trimeter**        four feet:  **tetrameter**
five feet:  **pentameter**      six feet:  **hexameter**

What are the lines in Wordsworth's poem called?

**Rhyme is the repetition of the same sound, usually at the end of lines.**

Poems do not necessarily have to rhyme but many do and older poems often have very fixed and interesting patterns of rhyme.

Rhymes of one syllable (a single sound) are easy.
For example: *bill – mill, fill, sill, kill, dill, will, hill, till, gill, Jill, nil, pill, quill.*

Rhymes where the last two syllables are the same are a little more difficult.
For example:*wedding – shedding, dreading, treading, bedding, threading, spreading.*

You might even like to try rhyming three syllables.
For example:*Needier – speedier, weedier, greedier, seedier, reedier, beadier.*

1    How many rhymes can you make for these words?
      *Air* (target 35); *bat* (target 25); *spying* (target 15); *showing* (target 20);
      *chattering* (target 8)

**You need to know...**
A Rhyming Couplet is simply two consecutive lines that rhyme.

2    This little poem is made up of eight rhyming couplets.
    The last word of each line has been left out.
    Use this list of the missing words to complete the poem so that it makes sense.

The missing words: *bleed, crack, weeds, grow, wall, smart, snow, back, indeed, roar, sky, heart, door, deeds, fall, fly.*

*A man of words and not of .........*
*Is like a garden full of ..........*
*When the weeds begin to .........,*
*It's like a garden full of .........;*
*When the snow begins to .........,*
*It's like a bird upon the .........;*
*When the bird begins to .........,*
*It's like an eagle in the .........;*

*When the sky begins to ..........,*
*It's like a lion at the .........;*
*When the door begins to .........,*
*It's like a whip across your .........;*
*When your back begins to .........,*
*It's like a penknife in your .........;*
*And when your heart begins to .........,*
*You're dead, you're dead, you're dead .......*
                        ANON

Sometimes when poets cannot find a word that rhymes exactly they will use one that almost rhymes, one that make a similar sound. This is called a **half rhyme.**
Here are some examples of half rhymes:

*And with the juice of this I'll streak her **eyes**,*
*And make her full of hateful fantasi**es**.*

*The skylark and **thrush**,*
*The birds of the **bush**,*

*The Gnat that sings his summer's **song***
*Poison gets from Slander's **tongue**.*

*A Horse misused upon the **road***
*Calls to Heaven for human **blood**.*

It is sometimes useful to be able to describe a **rhyming pattern**.
This is done like this:

| | | | |
|---|---|---|---|
| Good  people all, of every sort, | A | There was an Old Man with a beard, | A |
| Give ear unto my song; | B | Who said, 'It is just as I feared! | A |
| And if you find it wondrous short, | A | Two owls and a Hen, | B |
| It cannot hold you long. | B | Four Larks and a Wren | B |
| | | Have all built their nest in my beard!' | A |

| | | | |
|---|---|---|---|
| He clasps the crag with crooked hands: | A | Over the mountains | A |
| Close to the sun in lonely lands, | A | And over the waves, | B |
| Ringed with the azure world, he stands. | A | Under the fountains | A |
| | | And under the graves; | B |
| The wrinkled sea beneath him crawls; | B | Under floods that are deepest, | C |
| He watches from his mountain walls, | B | Which Neptune obey, | D |
| And like a thunderbolt he falls | B | Over rocks that are steepest, | C |
| | | Love will find out the way. | D |

These are two verses from quite a long poem by Lord Tennyson called 'The Lady of Shalott'.

Allowing for the odd **half rhyme** you should notice that both verses have the same rhyming pattern. It is quite usual for a poem to repeat the pattern in every verse.

| | |
|---|---|
| On either side the river lie | Willows whiten, aspens quiver, |
| Long fields of barley and of rye, | Little breezes dusk and shiver |
| That clothe the world and meet the sky; | Through the wave that runs for ever |
| And through the field the road runs by | By the island in the river |
| To many-towered Camelot; | Flowing down to Camelot. |
| And up and down the people go, | Four gray walls, and four gray towers, |
| Gazing where the lilies blow | Overlook a space of flowers, |
| Round an island there below, | And the silent isle imbowers |
| The island of Shalott. | The Lady of Shalott. |

You will find 'The Lady of Shalott' on page 19. It is a fine example of **a narrative poem** - one that tells a story. In this case it is a very romantic and rather sad story set in the time of King Arthur and the lost land of Camelot. The lady of the title leads a lonely life, confined to a tower room on an island in a river. Forbidden to look out of her window she spends all her time looking at reflections in a mirror as all of life passes her by; she weaves what she sees into a tapestry. One day, Sir Lancelot passes by and the lady is tempted to look directly out at reality, with tragic consequences.

Apart from being an excellent story 'The Lady of Shalott' is full of the most beautiful language and rich imagery.

## Hard-hearted Barbara Allen

*This ballad was a favourite song of the cowboys of America but it is believed to have originated in England in the seventeenth century.*

All in the merry month of May,
　　When green buds they were swelling,
Young Jimmy Grove on his death-bed lay
　　For love of Barbara Allen.

He sent his man unto her then,
　　To the town where she was dwelling:
"O haste and come to my master dear,
　　If your name be Barbara Allen."

Slowly, slowly she rose up,
　　And she came where he was lying:
And when she drew the curtain by,
　　Says, "Young man, I think you're dying."

"O it's I am sick, and very, very sick,
　　And it's all for Barbara Allen."
"O the better for me you'll never be,
　　Tho' your heart's blood were a-spilling!"

"O do you not mind, young man," she says,
　　"When the red wine you were filling,
That you made the healths go round and round,
　　And slighted Barbara Allen?"

He turned his face unto the wall,
　　And death with him was dealing:
"Adieu, adieu, my dear friends all;
　　Be kind to Barbara Allen."

As she was walking o'er the fields,
　　She heard the dead-bell knelling:
And every beat the dead-bell gave,
　　Cried, "Woe to Barbara Allen!"

"O mother, mother, make my bed,
　　To lay me down in sorrow.
My love has died for me today,
　　I'll die for him tomorrow."

## The Bailiff's Daughter of Islington  (Traditional)

*This ballad dates back to the seventeenth century, which is why you may find some of the spelling rather strange. At that time ballads were very popular and if you went to a fair or market it is likely that you would find someone singing these songs and offering them for sale, roughly printed on sheets of paper called broadsides. Thus the songs came to be known as broadside ballads.*

There was a youthe, and a well-beloved youthe,
    And he was a squire's son:
He loved the bayliffe's daughter deare,
    That lived in Islington.

Yet she was coye and would not believe,
    That he did love her soe,
Noe nor at any time would she
    Any countenance to him showe.

But when his friendes did understand
    His fond and foolish minde,
They sent him up to faire London
    An apprentice for to binde.

And he had been seven long yeares
    And never his love could see:
'Many a teare have I shed for her sake,
    When she little thought of mee.'

The all the maids of Islington
    Went forth to sport and playe,
All but the bayliffe's daughter deare;
    She secretly stole awaye.

She pulled off her gowne of greene,
    And put on ragged attire,
And to faire London she would go
    Her true love to enquire.

And as she went along the high road,
    The weather being hot and drye,
She sat her downe upon a green bank,
    And her true love came riding bye.

She started up with a colour soe redd,
    Catching hold of his bridle-reine;
'One penny, one penny, kind sir,' she sayd,
    'Will ease me of much paine.'

'Before I give you one penny, sweet-heart,
    Praye tell me where you were borne.'
'At Islington, kind sir,' sayd shee,
    'Where I have had many a scorne.'

'I prythee, sweet-heart, then tell to mee,
    O tell me whether you knowe
The bayliffe's daughter of Islington.'
    'She is dead,sir, long agoe.'

'If she be dead, then take my horse,
    My saddle and bridle also;
For I will into some farr countrye,
    Where noe man shall me knowe.'

'O staye, O staye, thou goodlye youthe,
    She standeth by thy side;
She is here alive, she is not dead,
    And readye to be thy bride.'

'O farewell griefe, and welcome joye,
    Ten thousand times therefore;
For nowe I have founde mine owne true love,
    Whom I thought I should never see more.'

## Sir Patrick Spens

*This is a traditional Scottish ballad of the eighteenth century. These border ballads, as they are called, are usually found written in broad dialect which makes it difficult for a non-Scot to understand. I have therefore, reluctantly, translated it into more modern English, but nothing can compare with hearing it read in its original form.*

The king sits in Dunfermline town
    Drinking the blood-red wine;
'O where will I get a skilful skipper
    To sail this ship of mine?'

Up and spoke an elder knight,
    Sat at the king's right knee:
'Sir Patrick Spens is the best sailor
    That ever sailed the sea.'

The king has written a broad letter
    And sealed it with his hand,
And sent it to Sir Patrick Spens
    Was walking on the strand.

'To Noroway, to Noroway,
  To Noroway o'er the foam;
The King's own daughter of Noroway,
  'Tis you must bring her home!'

The first line that Sir Patrick read,
  A loud laugh laughed he:
The next line that Sir Patrick read
  The tear blinded his eye.

'O who is this has done this deed,
  And told the king of me;
To send us out this time of year
  To sail upon the sea?

In wind or wet, in hail or sleet,
  Our ship must sail the foam
The King's daughter of Noroway
  'Tis we must fetch her home.

Make haste, make haste, my merry men all,
  Our good ship sails the morn.'
'O say not so my master dear
  I fear a deadly storm.

I saw the new moon late last night
  With the old moon in her arm;
And if we go to sea, master,
  I fear we'll come to harm.'

They had not sailed a league, a league,
  A league but barely three,
When the sky grew dark and the wind blew loud
  And angry grew the sea.

The anchor broke and the topmast split,
  It was such a deadly storm.
The waves came over the broken ship,
  Till all her sides were torn.

'Go fetch a web of the silken cloth,
  Another of the twine,
And wrap them into our ship's side,
  And let not the sea come in.'

They fetched a web of the silken cloth,
  Another of the twine,
And they wrapped them round that good ship's side,
  But still the sea came in.

O loath, loath were our good Scots lords,
  To wet their cork-heeled shoes
But long before the play was played
  They wet their hats above.

And many was the feather bed
  That floated on the foam;
And many was the good lord's son
  That never more came home.

O long, long, may the ladies sit
  With their fans into their hand
Before they'll see Sir Patrick Spens
  Come sailing to the strand!

O long, long, may the maidens stand
  With their gold combs in their hair,
A-waiting for their own dear loves!
  For them they'll see no more.

Half hour, half hour to Aberdour,
  'Tis fifty fathom deep;
And there lies Sir Patrick Spens,
  With the Scots lords at his feet.

*Epitaphs are lines of verse found on tombstones. Here are three rather amusing ones.*

## For a Dentist

Stranger! Approach this spot with gravity!
David Brown is filling his last cavity.

## For Uncle Peter Dan'els

Beneath this stone, a lump of clay,
  Lies Uncle Peter Dan'els'
Who, early in the month of May,
  Took off his winter flannels.

## For a Tired Woman

Here lies a poor woman who was always tired.
She lived in a house where help was not hired.
Her last words on earth were: 'Dear Friends I am going
Where washing ain't done, nor sweeping, nor sewing;
But everything there is exact to my wishes;
For where they don't eat there's no washing of dishes.
I'll be where loud anthems will always be ringing,
But, having no voice, I'll be clear of the singing.
Don't mourn for me now; don't mourn for me never –
I'm going to do nothing for ever and ever.'

## Narrative Verse

*Any poem that tells a story could be called narrative verse, including the ballads on the previous pages. The difference is that the ballads were originally songs whereas the poems in this section were written to be read, often aloud, in the days before radio and television. Narrative poems can deal with a great variety of subjects ranging from comic to tragic; they can vary in length from something that can be read in a few minutes to poems that are longer than some novels.*

## The Lady of Shalott by Alfred, Lord Tennyson

On either side the river lie
Long fields of barley and of rye,
That clothe the wold and meet the sky;
And thro' the field the road runs by
To many-towered Camelot;
And up and down the people go,
Gazing where the lilies blow
Round an island there below,
The island of Shalott.

Willows whiten, aspens quiver,
Little breezes dusk and shiver
Thro' the wave that runs for ever
By the island in the river
Flowing down to Camelot.
Four grey walls and four grey towers,
Overlook a space of flowers,
And the silent isle embowers
The Lady of Shalott.

By the margin, willow-veiled,
Slide the heavy barges trailed
By slow horses; and unhailed
The shallop flitteth silken-sailed
Skimming down to Camelot:
But who hath seen her wave her hand?
Or at the casement seen her stand?
Or is she known in all the land,
The Lady of Shalott?

Only reapers, reaping early
In among the bearded barley,
Hear a song that echoes cheerly
From the river winding clearly,
Down to towered Camelot:
And by the moon the reaper weary,
Piling sheaves in uplands airy,
Listening, whispers ''Tis the fairy
Lady of Shalott'.

**Part 2**

*There she weaves by night and day*
*A magic web with colours gay.*
*She has heard a whisper say,*
*A curse is on her if she stay*
*To look down to Camelot.*
*She knows not what the curse may be,*
*And so she weaveth steadily,*
*And little other care hath she,*
*The Lady of Shalott.*

*And moving thro' a mirror clear*
*That hangs before her all the year,*
*Shadows of the world appear.*
*There she sees the highway near*
*Winding down to Camelot:*
*There the river eddy whirls,*
*And there the surly village churls,*
*And the red cloaks of market girls,*
*Pass onward from Shalott.*

*Sometimes a troop of damsels glad,*
*An abbot on an ambling pad,*
*Sometimes a curly shepherd lad,*
*Or long-haired page in crimson clad,*
*Goes by to towered Camelot:*
*And sometimes thro' the mirror blue*
*The knights come riding two by two:*
*She hath no loyal knight and true,*
*The Lady of Shalott.*

*But in her web she still delights*
*To weave the mirror's magic sights,*
*For often thro' the silent nights*
*A funeral, with plumes and lights,*
*And music, went to Camelot:*
*Or when the moon was overhead,*
*Came two young lovers lately wed:*
*'I am half sick of shadows,' said*
*The Lady of Shalott.*

**Part 3**

A bow-shot from her bower-eaves,
He rode between the barley sheaves,
The sun came dazzling thro' the leaves,
And flamed upon the brazen greaves
Of bold Sir Lancelot.
A red-cross knight for ever kneeled
To a lady in his shield,
That sparkled on the yellow field,
Beside remote Shalott.

The gemmy bridle glittered free,
Like to some branch of stars we see
Hung in the golden Galaxy.
The bridle bells rang merrily
As he rode down to Camelot:
And from his blazoned baldric slung
A mighty silver bugle hung,
And as he rode his armour rung,
Beside remote Shalott.

All in the blue unclouded weather
Thick-jewelled shone the saddle-leather,
The helmet and the helmet-feather
Burned like one burning flame together,
As he rode down to Camelot.
As often thro' the purple night,
Below the starry clusters bright,
Some bearded meteor, trailing light,
Moves over still Shalott.

His broad clear brow in sunlight glowed;
On burnished hooves his war-horse trode;
From underneath his helmet flowed
His coal-black curls as on he rode,
As he rode down to Camelot.
From the bank and from the river
He flashed into the crystal mirror,
'Tirra lirra,' by the river
Sang Sir Lancelot.

She left the web, she left the loom,
She made three paces thro' the room,
She saw the water-lily bloom,
She saw the helmet and the plume,
She looked down to Camelot.
Out flew the web and floated wide;
The mirror cracked from side to side;
'The curse is come upon me,' cried
The Lady of Shalott.

**Part 4**

*In the stormy east wind straining,*
*The pale yellow woods were waning,*
*The broad stream in his banks complaining,*
*Heavily the low sky raining*
*Over towered Camelot.*
*Down she came and found a boat*
*Beneath a willow left afloat,*
*And round about the prow she wrote*
*'The Lady of Shalott'.*

*And down the river's dim expanse-*
*Like some bold seer in a trance,*
*Seeing all his own mischance-*
*With a glassy countenance*
*Did she look to Camelot.*
*And at the closing of the day*
*She loosed the chain and down she lay;*
*The broad stream bore her far away,*
*The Lady of Shalott.*

*Lying, robed in snowy white*
*That loosely flew to left and right-*
*The leaves upon her falling light-*
*Thro' the noises of the night*
*She floated down to Camelot:*
*And as the boat-head wound along*
*The willowy hills and fields among,*
*They heard her singing her last song,*
*The Lady of Shalott.*

*Heard a carol, mournful, holy,*
*Chanted loudly, chanted lowly,*
*Till her blood was frozen slowly,*
*And her eyes were darkened wholly,*
*Turned to towered Camelot;*
*For ere she reached upon the tide*
*The first house by the waterside,*
*Singing in her song, she died,*
*The Lady of Shalott.*

*Under tower and balcony,*
*By garden wall and gallery,*
*A gleaming shape she floated by,*
*Dead-pale between the houses high,*
*Silent into Camelot.*
*Out upon the wharfs they came,*
*Knight and burgher, lord and dame,*
*And round the prow they read her name,*
*'The Lady of Shalott'.*

Who is this? and what is here?
And in the lighted palace near
Died the sound of royal cheer;
And they crossed themselves for fear,
All the knights at Camelot:
But Lancelot mused a little space;
He said, 'She has a lovely face;
God in his mercy lend her grace,
The Lady of Shalott.'

## The Wreck of the Hesperus by Henry Wadsworth Longfellow

It was the schooner Hesperus
    That sailed the wintry sea;
And the skipper had taken his little daughter,
    To bear him company.

Blue were her eyes as the fairy-flax,
    Her cheeks like the dawn of day,
And her bosom white as the hawthorn buds
    That ope in the month of May.

The skipper he stood beside the helm,
    His pipe was in his mouth,
And he watched how the veering flaw did blow
    The smoke now west, now south.

Then up and spake an old sailor,
    Had sailed the Spanish Main,
'I pray thee, put into yonder port,
    For I fear a hurricane.

'Last night the moon had a golden ring,
    And tonight no moon we see!'
The skipper he blew a whiff from his pipe,
    And a scornful laugh laughed he.

Colder and louder blew the wind,
    A gale from the north-east,
The snow fell hissing in the brine,
    And the billows frothed like yeast.

Down came the storm, and smote amain
    The vessel in its strength;
She shuddered and paused like a frighted steed,
    Then leaped her cable's length.

'Come hither! come hither! my little daughter,
    And do not tremble so;
For I can weather the roughest gale
    That ever wind did blow.'

He wrapped her warm in his seaman's coat
    Against the stinging blast;
He cut a rope from a broken spar,
    And bound her to the mast.

'O father! I hear the church bells ring,
    O say, what may it be?'
'Some ship in distress, that cannot live
    In such an angry sea!'

'O father! I see a gleaming light,
    O say, what may it be?'
But the father answered never a word,
    A frozen corpse was he.

Lashed to the helm, all stiff and stark,
    With his face turned to the skies,
The lantern gleamed through the gleaming snow
    On his fixed and glassy eyes.

Then the maiden clasped her hands and prayed
    That savéd she might be;
And she thought of Christ, who stilled the wave
    On the Lake of Galilee.

And fast through the midnight dark and drear,
    Through the whistling sleet and snow,
Like a sheeted ghost the vessel swept
    Towards the reef of Norman's Woe.

And ever the fitful gusts between
    A sound came from the land;
It was the sound of the trampling surf
    On the rocks and the hard sea-sand.

The breakers were right beneath her bows,
    She drifted a dreary wreck,
And a whooping billow swept the crew
    Like icicles from her deck.

She struck where the white and fleecy waves
    Looked soft as carded wool,
But the cruel rocks they gored her side
    Like the horns of an angry bull.

Her rattling shrouds, all sheathed in ice,
    With the masts went by the board;
Like a vessel of glass she stove and sank –
    Ho! Ho! The breakers roared!

At daybreak on the bleak sea-beach
    A fisherman stood aghast,
To see the form of a maiden fair
    Lashed close to a drifting mast.

The salt sea was frozen on her breast,
    The salt tears in her eyes;
And he saw her hair, like the brown sea-weed,
    On the billows fall and rise.

Such was the wreck of the Hesperus,
    In the midnight and the snow!
Christ save us all from a death like this,
    On the reef of Norman's Woe!

## The Lion and Albert by Marriott Edgar

There's a famous seaside place called Blackpool,
    That's noted for fresh air and fun,
And Mr and Mrs Ramsbottom
    Went there with young Albert, their son.

A grand little lad was young Albert,
    All dressed in his best; quite a swell
With a stick with an 'orse's 'ead 'andle,
    The finest that Woolworth's could sell.

They didn't think much to the Ocean:
    The waves, they was fiddlin' and small,
There was no wrecks and nobody drownded,
    Fact, nothing to laugh at at all.

So, seeking for further amusement,
    They paid and went into the Zoo,
Where they'd Lions and Tigers and Camels,
    And old ale and sandwiches too.

There was one great big Lion called Wallace;
    His nose were all covered in scars-
He lay in a somnolent posture
    With the side of his face on the bars.

Now Albert had heard about Lions,
    How they was ferocious and wild-
To see Wallace lying so peaceful,
    Well, it didn't seem right to the child.

So straightway the brave little feller,
    Not showing a morsel of fear,
Took his stick with its 'orse's 'ead 'andle
    And pushed it in Wallace's ear.

You could see that the Lion didn't like it,
    For giving a kind of a roll,
He pulled Albert inside the cage with 'im,
    And swallowed the little lad 'ole.

Then Pa, who had seen the occurrence,
    And didn't know what to do next,
Said 'Mother! Yon Lion's 'et Albert,'
    And Mother said 'Well I am vexed!'

Then Mr and Mrs Ramsbottom-
    Quite rightly, when all's said and done-
Complained to the Animal Keeper
    That the Lion had eaten their son.

The keeper was quite nice about it;
    He said 'What a nasty mishap.
Are you sure that it's **your** boy he's eaten?'
    Pa said 'Am I sure?  There's his cap!'

The manager had to be sent for.
    He came and he said 'What's to do?'
Pa said 'Yon Lion's 'et Albert,
    And 'im in his Sunday clothes, too.'

Then Mother said, 'Right's right, young feller;
    I think it's a shame and a sin
For a lion to go and eat Albert,
    And after we've paid to come in.'

The manager wanted no trouble,
    He took out his purse right away,
Saying 'How much to settle the matter?'
    And Pa said 'What do you usually pay?'

But Mother had turned a bit awkward
    When she thought where her Albert had gone.
She said 'No! someone's got to be summonsed'-
    So that was decided upon.

Then off they went to the P'lice Station,
    In front of the Magistrate chap;
They told 'im what happened to Albert,
    And proved it by showing his cap.

The Magistrate gave his opinion
    That no one was really to blame
And he said that he hoped the Ramsbottoms
    Would have further sons to their name.

At that Mother got proper blazing,
    'And thank you, sir, kindly,' said she.
'What waste all our lives raising children
    To feed ruddy Lions?  Not me!'

**The Burial of Sir John Moore after Corunna by Charles Wolfe**

Not a drum was heard, not a funeral note,
    As his corse to the rampart we hurried;
Not a soldier discharged his farewell shot
    O'er the grave where our hero we buried.

We buried him darkly at dead of night,
    The sods with our bayonets turning;
By the struggling moonbeam's misty light,
    And the lantern dimly burning.

No useless coffin enclosed his breast,
    Not in sheet or in shroud we wound him;
But he lay like a warrior taking his rest,
    With his martial cloak around him.

Few and short were the prayers we said,
    And we spoke not a word of sorrow;
But we steadfastly gazed on the face that was dead,
    And we bitterly thought of the morrow.

We thought, as we hollowed his narrow bed,
    And smoothed down his lonely pillow,
That the foe and the stranger would tread o'er his head,
    And we far away on the billow!

Lightly they'll talk of the spirit that's gone,
    And o'er his cold ashes upbraid him. –
But little he'll reck*, if they let him sleep on                *care
    In the grave where a Briton has laid him.

But half of our heavy task was done
    When the clock struck the hour for retiring;
And we heard the distant and random gun
    That the foe was sullenly firing.

Slowly and sadly we laid him down,
    From the field of his fame fresh and gory;
We carved not a line and we raised not a stone –
    But we left him alone with his glory.


## Little Billee by W. M. Thackeray

There were three sailors of Bristol city
Who took a boat and went to sea.
But first with beef and captain's biscuits
And pickled pork they loaded she.

There was gorging Jack and guzzling Jimmy,
And the youngest he was little Billee.
Now when they got as far as the Equator
They'd nothing left but one split pea.

Says gorging Jack to guzzling Jimmy,
'I am extremely hungaree.'
To gorging Jack says guzzling Jimmy,
'We've nothing left, us must eat we.'

Says gorging Jack to guzzling Jimmy,
'With one another we shouldn't agree!
There's little Bill, he's young and tender,
We're old and tough, so let's eat he.'

'Oh! Billee, we're going to kill and eat you,
So undo the button of your chemie.'
When Bill received this information
He used his pocket handkerchie.

'First, let me say my catechism,
Which my poor mammy taught to me.'
'Make haste, make haste,' says guzzling Jimmy,
While Jack pulled out his snickersnee.

So Billee went up to the main-top gallant mast,
And down he fell on his bended knee.
He scarce had come to the twelfth commandment
When up he jumps, 'There's land I see:

*'Jerusalem and Madagascar,*
*And North and South Amerikee:*
*There's the British flag a-riding at anchor,*
*With Admiral Napier, K.C.B.'*

*So when they got aboard of the Admiral's,*
*He hanged fat Jack and flogged Jimmee;*
*But as for little Bill he made him*
*The Captain of a Seventy-three.*


*If you have enjoyed reading these stories – because that is what narrative poems are, stories –
here are some suggestions of other famous poems of the same kind that you should be able to
find without too much difficulty.*

'The Jackdaw of Rheims'               by      Richard Harris Barham

'The Pied Piper of Hamelin'           by      Robert Browning

'Morte d'Arthur' ('Death of Arthur')  by      Lord Alfred Tennyson

'The Rime of the Ancient Mariner'     by      Samuel Taylor Coleridge

'The Hunting of the Snark'            by      Lewis Carroll

'Horatius'                            by      Lord  Macaulay

'Hiawatha'                            by      H. W. Longfellow

'Growltiger's Last Stand'             by      T. S. Eliot

'The Raven'                           by      Edgar Allan Poe

## Odes

*The word 'Ode' is derived from a Greek word meaning 'song', but unlike the ballads that we have already looked at, odes are invariably serious and far more structured. English poets, including Keats and Shelley, Wordsworth, Coleridge and Tennyson, all wrote numerous odes but they departed from the very rigid form of the original Greek choral ode. However, what they wrote still contains very disciplined patterns. Odes also tend to be rather long and therefore I have included here only a few sample verses. What I hope you will notice is the wonderfully rich language and imagery that they contain. The Odes writtten by poets of the past represent some of the finest poetry in the English language.*

### from **Ode to a Nightingale** by **John Keats**

*(This is the fifth of eight ten-lined verses. The same rhyming pattern of abab cde cde is followed in every verse)*

> I cannot see what flowers are at my feet,
> 　　Nor what soft incense hangs upon the boughs,
> But in embalmèd darkness, guess each sweet
> 　　Wherewith the seasonable month endows
> The grass, the thicket, and the fruit-tree wild;
> 　　White hawthorn, and the pastoral eglantine;
> 　　Fast-fading violets cover'd up in leaves;
> 　　　　And mid-May's eldest child,
> The coming musk-rose, full of dewy wine,
> 　　The murmurous haunt of flies on summer eves.

### From **Ode to the West Wind** by **Percy Bysshe Shelley**

*(This is the first of five parts, each part composed of 5 stanzas of 3,3,3,3 and 2 lines with a complex rhyming pattern of: a b a – b c b – c d c – d e d – f f)*

> O Wild West Wind, thou breath of Autumn's being
> 　　Thou from whose unseen presence the leaves dead
> Are driven like ghosts from an enchanter fleeing,
>
> 　　Yellow, and black, and pale, and hectic red,
> Pestilence-stricken multitudes! O thou
> 　　Who chariotest to their dark wintry bed
>
> The wingèd seeds, where they lie cold and low,
> 　　Each like a corpse within its grave, until
> Thine azure sister of the Spring shall blow
>
> 　　Her clarion o'er the dreaming earth, and fill
> (Driving sweet buds like flocks to feed in air)
> 　　With living hues and odours plain and hill;
>
> Wild Spirit, which art moving everywhere;
> Destroyer and preserver; hear, O hear!

# Elegies

*The elegy is similar in many ways to the ode but the subject is always mournful, reflecting on the death of a friend or some great figure or the passing of something that is forever lost.*

## O Captain! My Captain! by Walt Whitman

*Walt Whitman was one of the most important American poets, whose popularity remains even today. In this poem Whitman's Captain /Father is his President, Abraham Lincoln, who was assassinated in 1874 following his successful fight against slavery in the American Civil War ("the prize we fought is won"). The 'ship' is the ship of state, his country, united at last.*

O Captain! my Captain! our fearful trip is done,
The ship has weather'd every rack, the prize we sought is won,
The port is near, the bells I hear, the people all exulting,
While follow eyes the steady keel, the vessel grim and daring;
        But O heart! heart! heart!
        O the bleeding drops of red!
            Where on the deck my Captain lies,
                Fallen cold and dead.

O Captain! my Captain! rise up and hear the bells;
Rise up – for you the flag is flung – for you the bugle trills,
For you bouquets and ribbon'd wreaths – for you the shores crowding,
For you they call, the swaying mass, their eager faces turning;
        Here, Captain! dear father!
        This arm beneath your head!
            It is some dream that on the deck
                You've fallen cold and dead.

My Captain does not answer, his lips are pale and still,
My father does not feel my arm, he has no pulse nor will;
The ship is anchor'd safe and sound, its voyage closed and done,
From fearful trip the victor ship comes in with object won;
        Exult ,O shores! and sing, O bells!
        But I, with mournful tread,
            Walk the deck my Captain lies,
                Fallen cold and dead.

from **Elegy written in a Country Churchyard** by **Thomas Gray**

*The curfew tolls the knell of parting day,*
*The lowing herd wind slowly o'er the lea,*
*The plowman homeward plods his weary way,*
*And leaves the world to darkness and to me.*

*Now fades the glimmering landscape on the sight,*
*And all the air a solemn stillness holds,*
*Save where the beetle wheels his droning flight,*
*And drowsy tinklings lull the distant folds;*

*Save that from yonder ivy-mantled tower*
*The moping owl does to the moon complain*
*Of such as, wand'ring near her secret bower,*
*Molest her ancient solitary reign.*

*Beneath those rugged elms, that yew-tree's shade,*
*Where heaves the turf in many a mould'ring heap,*
*Each in his narrow cell for ever laid,*
*The rude Forefathers of the hamlet sleep.*

from **In Memoriam** by **Alfred, Lord Tennyson**
*Tennyson wrote this long poem on the death of his friend Arthur Hallam.*

*Now fades the last long streak of snow,*
*Now burgeons every maze of quick*
*About the flowering squares, and thick*
*By ashen roots the violets blow.*

*Now rings the woodland loud and long,*
*The distance takes a lovelier hue,*
*And drown'd in yonder living blue,*
*The lark becomes a sightless song.*

*Now dance the lights on lawn and lea,*
*The flocks are whiter down the vale,*
*And milkier every milky sail*
*On winding stream or distant sea;*

*Where now the seamew pipes, or dives*
*In yonder greening gleam, and fly*
*The happy birds that change their sky*
*To build and brood; that live their lives*

*From land to land; and in my breast*
*Spring wakens too; and my regret*
*Becomes an April violet*
*And buds and blossoms like the rest.*

## Epigrams

What is an epigram?  A dwarfish whole,
Its body brevity, and wit its soul.

**Samuel Taylor Coleridge**

Her whole life is an epigram, smart, smooth and neatly penn'd,
Platted quite neat to catch applause with a sliding noose at the end.

**William Blake**

## Misfortunes never come Singly

Making toast at the fireside,
Nurse fell in the grate and died:
And what makes it ten times worse,
All the toast was burnt with nurse.

**Harry Graham**

## Bibo – An Epigram

When BIBO thought fit from the world to retreat,
As full of Champagne as an egg's full of meat,
He wak'd in the boat; and to CHARON he said,
He wou'd be row'd back, for he was not yet dead.
Trim the boat, and sit quiet, stern CHARON reply'd:
You may have forgot, you were drunk when you died.

**Matthew Prior**

## Epigram
*engraved on the collar of a dog which I gave to his Royal Highness Frederick Prince of Wales*

I am his Highness' dog at Kew.
Pray tell me, sir, whose dog are you?

**Alexander Pope**

## Extempore
*On the death of Edward Purdon*

Here lies poor Ned Purdon, from misery freed,
Who long was a bookseller's hack;
He led such a damnable life in this world,
I don't think he'll ever come back.

**Oliver Goldsmith**

## Tender Heartedness

Billy, in one of his nice new sashes,
Fell in the fire and was burnt to ashes:
Now, although the room grows chilly,
I haven't the heart to poke poor Billy.

**Harry Graham**

**Sonnets**

### Sonnet 18 by **William Shakespeare**

> Shall I compare thee to a summer's day?
> Thou art more lovely and more temperate:
> Rough winds do shake the darling buds of May,
> And summer's lease hath all too short a date:
> Sometime too hot the eye of heaven shines,
> And often is his gold complexion dimm'd,
> And every fair from fair sometime declines,
> By chance or nature's changing course untrimm'd:
> But thy eternal summer shall not fade,
> Nor lose possession of that fair thou ow'st;
> Nor shall death brag thou wandrest in his shade,
> When in eternal lines to time thou growest.
>      So long as men can breathe or eyes can see
> So long lives this, and this gives life to thee.

### Composed upon Westminster Bridge by **William Wordsworth**

> Earth has not anything to show more fair:
>      Dull would he be of soul who could pass by
>      A sight so touching in its majesty:
> This City now doth like a garment wear
>
> The beauty of the morning; silent, bare,
>      Ships, towers, domes, theatres, and temples lie
>      Open unto the fields, and to the sky;
> All bright and glittering in the smokeless air.
>
> Never did sun more beautifully steep
>      In his first splendour, valley, rock, or hill;
> Ne'er saw I, never felt, a calm so deep!
>      The river glideth at his own sweet will:
> Dear God! The very houses seem asleep;
>      And all that mighty heart is lying still!

## Sonnet from the Portuguese XLIII by **Elizabeth Barrett Browning**

*Elizabeth Barrett Browning is generally recognised to be the foremost woman poet of her age. Her life was in many ways tragic and has been the subject of books, plays and films. She married the poet Robert Browning, to whom she wrote this poem of love.*

How do I love thee? Let me count the ways.
    I love thee to the depth and breadth and height
    My soul can reach, when feeling out of sight
For the ends of Being and ideal Grace.
I love thee to the level of everyday's
    Most quiet need, by sun and candlelight.
    I love thee freely, as men strive for Right;
I love thee purely, as they turn from Praise.
I love thee with the passion put to use
    In my old griefs, and with my childhood's faith.
I love thee with a love I seemed to lose
    With my lost saints, - I love thee with the breath,
Smiles, tears, of all my life! - and, if God choose,
    I shall but love thee better after death.

*It is interesting to note that the writers of the following three sonnets all died young. The first two died in the First World War, Rupert Brooke aged 28 and Wilfred Owen at 21. The young pilot, John Gillespie Magee died in 1942 when he was just 19.*

## The Soldier by **Rupert Brooke**

If I should die, think only this of me:
    That there's some corner of a foreign field
That is for ever England. There shall be
    In that rich earth a richer dust concealed;
A dust whom England bore, shaped, made aware,
    Gave, once, her flowers to love, her ways to roam,
A body of England's, breathing English air,
    Washed by the rivers, blest by suns of home.
And think, this heart, all evil shed away,
    A pulse in the eternal mind, no less
    Gives somewhere back the thoughts by England given;
Her sights and sounds; dreams happy as her day;
    And laughter, learnt of friends; and gentleness,
    In hearts at peace, under an English heaven.

## Anthem for Doomed Youth by Wilfred Owen

What passing bells for those who die as cattle?
    Only the monstrous anger of the guns.
Only the stuttering rifles' rapid rattle
    Can patter out their hasty orisons.
No mockeries now for them; no prayers nor bells,
    Nor any voice of mourning save the choirs,-
The shrill, demented choirs of wailing shells;
    And bugles calling for them from sad shires.

What candles may be held to speed them all?
    Not in the hands of boys, but in their eyes
Shall shine the holy glimmers of good-byes.
    The pallor of girls' brows shall be their pall;
Their flowers the tenderness of patient minds,
And each slow dusk a drawing-down of blinds.

## High Flight (An Airman's Ecstasy) by John Gillespie Magee

Oh, I have slipped the surly bonds of earth
    And danced the skies on laughter-silvered wings;
Sunward I've climbed and joined the tumbling mirth
    Of sun-split clouds – and done a hundred things
You have not dreamed of; wheeled and soared and swung
    High in the sun-lit silence. Hovering there
I've chased the shouting wind along, and flung
    My eager craft through footless halls of air;
Up, up the long, delirious, burning blue
    I've topped the wind-swept heights with easy grace,
Where never lark nor even eagle flew;
And while, with silent lifting mind I've trod
    The high untrespassed sanctity of space,
Put out my hand, and touched the face of God.

## Haiku

A flitting firefly.
Look!  Look there! I start to call.
But there is no-one.

**Taigi**

The grasshoppers' cry
Does not reveal how very
Soon they are to die.

**Basho**

Dew in the rouge-flower
Shines like a great red jewel.
Spilled, only water.

**Kaga no Chiyo**

At the butterflies
The caged bird looks in envy.
Sadness in his eyes.

**Issa**

The Autumn leaves fall.
Fall and pile up while the rain
Falls upon the rain.

**Gyodai**

Snow begins to melt
And the village overflows
With many children.

**Issa**

## Clerihews

Jonathan Swift
Never went up in a lift;
Nor did the author of 'Robinson Crusoe'
Do so.

**Anon.**

Geoffrey Chaucer
Always drank out of a saucer.
He said it made him feel such an ass
To drink out of a glass.

**Anon.**

## Parody

*Read this poem by Robert Southey and then read 'You Are Old Father William' by Lewis Carroll on the opposite page and you will understand what is meant by the word 'Parody'*

## The Old Man's Comforts, and How He Gained Them by Robert Southey

You are old, Father William, the young man cried,
    The few locks that are left you are gray;
You are hale, Father William, a hearty old man,
    Now tell me the reason, I pray.

In the days of my youth, Father William replied,
    I remember'd that youth would fly fast,
And abused not my health and my vigour at first,
    That I never might need them at last.

You are old, Father William, the young man cried,
    And pleasures with youth pass away,
And yet you lament not the days that are gone,
    Now tell me the reason, I pray.

In the days of my youth, Father William replied,
    I remember'd that youth could not last;
I thought of the future, whatever I did,
    That I never might grieve for the past.

You are old, Father William, the young man cried,
    And life must be hastening away;
You are cheerful, and love to converse upon death!
    Now tell me the reason, I pray.

I am cheerful, young man, Father William replied;
    Let the cause thy attention engage;
In the days of my youth, I remember'd my God!
    And He hath not forgotten my age.

## You Are Old, Father William by Lewis Carroll

'You are old, Father William,' the young man said,
   'And your hair has become very white;
And yet you incessantly stand on your head -
   Do you think, at your age, it is right?'

'In my youth,' Father William replied to his son,
   'I feared it might injure the brain;
But now that I'm perfectly sure I have none,
   Why, I do it again and again.'

'You are old,' said the youth, 'as I mentioned before,
   And have grown most uncommonly fat;
Yet you turned a back-somersault in at the door -
   Pray, what is the reason of that?'

'In my youth,' said the sage, as he shook his grey locks,
   'I kept all my limbs very supple
By the use of this ointment - one shilling the box -
   Allow me to sell you a couple.'

'You are old,' said the youth, 'and your jaws are too weak
   For anything tougher than suet;
Yet you finished the goose, with the bones and the beak -
   Pray, how did you manage to do it?'

'In my youth,' said his father, 'I took to the law,
   And argued each case with my wife;
And the muscular strength which it gave to my jaw
   Has lasted the rest of my life.'

'You are old,' said the youth; 'one would hardly suppose
   That your eye was as steady as ever;
Yet you balanced an eel on the end of your nose -
   What made you so awfully clever?'

'I have answered three questions, and that is enough,'
   Said his father; 'don't give yourself airs!
Do you think I can listen all day to such stuff?
   Be off, or I'll kick you down stairs!'

## Poems about People

### The Little Dancers by Laurence Binyon

> Lonely, save for a few faint stars, the sky
> Dreams; and lonely, below, the little street
> Into its gloom retires, secluded and shy.
> Scarcely the dumb roar enters this soft retreat;
> And all is dark, save where come flooding rays
> From a tavern window; there, to the brisk measure
> Of an organ that down in an alley merrily plays,
> Two children, all alone and no one by,
> Holding their tattered frocks, thro' an airy maze
> Of motion lightly threaded with nimble feet
> Dance sedately; face to face they gaze,
> Their eyes shining, grave with a perfect pleasure.

### At the Railway Station, Upwey by Thomas Hardy

> 'There is not much that I can do,
>     For I've no money that's quite my own!'
>     Spoke up the pitying child –
> A little boy with a violin
> At the station before the train came in, -
> 'But I can play my fiddle to you,
> And a nice one 'tis, and good in tone!'
>
> The man in the handcuffs smiled;
> The constable looked, and he smiled too,
>     As the fiddle began to twang;
> And the man in the handcuffs suddenly sang
>     With grimful glee:
>     'This life so free
>     Is the thing for me!'
> And the constable smiled, and said no word,
> As if unconscious of what he heard;
> And so they went on till the train came in –
> The convict, and boy with the violin.

### There was a Young Man of Bengal (Anon)

> There was a young man of Bengal
> Who went to a fancy-dress ball.
> He went just for fun
> Dressed up as a bun
> But a dog ate him up in the hall.

## Meg Merrilies by John Keats

Old Meg she was a Gypsy
 And liv'd upon the Moors:
Her bed it was the brown heath turf,
 And her house was out of doors.

Her apples were swart blackberries,
 Her currants pods o' broom;
Her wine was dew o' the wild white rose
 Her book a churchyard tomb.

Her Brothers were the craggy hills,
 Her Sisters larchen trees –
Alone with her great family
 She liv'd as she did please.

No breakfast had she many a morn,
 No dinner many a noon,
And 'stead of supper she would stare
 Full hard against the Moon.

But every morn of woodbine fresh
 She made her garlanding,
And every night the dark glen Yew
 She wove, and she would sing.

And with her fingers old and brown
 She plaited Mats o' Rushes,
And gave them to the Cottagers
 She met among the Bushes.

Old Meg was brave as Margaret Queen
 And tall as Amazon:
An old red blanket cloak she wore;
 A chip hat had she on.
God rest her aged bones somewhere –
 She died full long agone!

## Solomon Grundy (Anon)

Solomon Grundy,
 Born on a Monday,
  Christened on Tuesday,
   Married on Wednesday,
    Took ill on Thursday,
   Worse on Friday,
  Died on Saturday,
 Buried on Sunday.
This is the end of Solomon Grundy.

**Poems about Places**

**I Remember, I Remember by Thomas Hood**

I remember, I remember
    The house where I was born,
The little window where the sun
    Came peeping in at morn:
He never came a wink too soon,
    Nor brought too long a day, -
But now, I often wish the night
    Had borne my breath away!

I remember, I remember
    The roses, red and white,
The violets and the lily cups –
    Those flowers made of light!
The lilacs where the robin built
    And where my brother set
The laburnum on his birthday, -
    The tree is living yet!

I remember, I remember
    Where I was used to swing,
And thought the air must rush as fresh
    To swallows on the wing:
My spirit flew in feathers then,
    That is so heavy now, -
And summer pools could hardly cool
    The fever on my brow!

I remember, I remember
    The fir-trees dark and high;
I used to think their slender tops
    Were close against the sky.
It was a childish ignorance,
    But now 'tis little joy
To know I'm further off from Heaven
    Than when I was a boy.

## The Way Through the Woods by **Rudyard Kipling**

They shut the road through the woods
    Seventy years ago.
Weather and rain have undone it again,
    And now you would never know
There was once a road through the woods
    Before they planted the trees.
It is underneath the coppice and heath
    And the thin anemones.
    Only the keeper sees
That where the ring-dove broods,
    And the badgers roll at ease
There was once a road through the woods.

Yet, if you enter the woods
    Of a summer evening late,
When the night-air cools on the trout-ringed pools
    Where the otter whistles his mate,
(They fear not men in the woods,
    Because they see so few.)
You will hear the beat of a horse's feet,
    And the swish of a skirt in the dew,
    Steadily cantering through
The misty solitudes,
    As though they perfectly knew
The old lost road through the woods ...
But there is no road through the woods.


## The Lake Isle of Innisfree by **W. B. Yeats**

I will arise and go now, and go to Innisfree,
And a small cabin build there, of clay and wattles made:
Nine bean-rows will I have there, a hive for the honey-bee,
    And live alone in the bee-loud glade.

And I shall have some peace there, for peace comes dropping slow,
Dropping from the veils of the morning to where the cricket sings;
There midnight's all a glimmer, and noon a purple glow,
    And evening full of the linnet's wings.

I will arise and go now, for always night and day
I hear lake water lapping with low sounds by the shore;
While I stand on the roadway, or on the pavements grey,
    I hear it in the deep heart's core.

## Home Thoughts, from Abroad by **Robert Browning**

O to be in England
Now that April's there,
And whoever wakes in England
Sees, some morning, unaware,
That the lowest boughs and the brushwood sheaf
Round the elm-tree bole are in tiny leaf,
While the chaffinch sings on the orchard bough
In England – now!

And after April, when May follows,
And the whitethroat builds, and all the swallows!
Hark, where my blossom'd pear-tree in the hedge
Leans to the field and scatters on the clover
Blossoms and dewdrops – at the bent spray's edge -
That's the wise thrush; he sings each song twice over
Lest you should think he never could recapture
The first fine careless rapture!
And though the fields look rough with hoary dew,
All will be gay when noontide wakes anew
The buttercups, the little children's dower
- Far brighter than this gaudy melon-flower!


## Symphony in Yellow by **Oscar Wilde**

An omnibus across the bridge
    Crawls like a yellow butterfly,
    And, here and there, a passer-by
Shows like a little restless midge.

Big barges full of yellow hay
    Are moored against the shadowy wharf,
    And, like a yellow silken scarf,
The thick fog hangs along the quay.

The yellow leaves begin to fade
    And flutter from the Temple elms,
    And at my feet the pale green Thames
Lies like a rod of rippled jade.

## The Big Rock Candy Mountains (Anon.)

One evenin' as the sun went down
And the jungle fire was burnin',
Down the track came a hobo hikin',
And he said: 'Boys, I'm not turnin',
I'm headed fer a land that's far away
Beside the crystal fountains,
So come with me, we'll all go see
    The Big Rock Candy Mountains.

'In the Big Rock Candy Mountains
There's a land that's fair and bright,
Where the handouts grow on bushes,
And you sleep out every night.
Where the boxcars are all empty,
And the sun shines every day
On the birds and the bees and the cigarette trees,
And the lemonade springs where the bluebird sings
    In the Big Rock Candy Mountains.

'In the Big Rock Candy Mountains,
All the cops have wooden legs,
The bulldogs all have rubber teeth,
And the hens lay soft-boiled eggs.
The farmers' trees are full of fruit,
And the barns are full of hay.
Oh, I'm bound to go where there ain't no snow,
Where the rain don't pour, the wind don't blow.
    In the Big Rock Candy Mountains.

'In the Big Rock Candy Mountains,
You never change your socks,
And the little streams of alcohol
Come tricklin' down the rocks.
There the brakemen have to tip their hats
And the railroad bulls are blind.
There's a lake of stew and of whiskey too,
You can paddle all around 'em in a big canoe,
    In the Big Rock Candy Mountains.

'In the Big Rock Candy Mountains,
All the jails are made of tin,
And you can bust right out again
As soon as you are in.
There ain't no short-handled shovels,
No axes, saws or picks.
I'm going to stay where you sleep all day,
Where they hung the Turk that invented work,
    In the Big Rock Candy Mountains.

**Descriptive Verse**

**The Cataract of Lodore** by **Robert Southey**

*You will rarely find a poem with more internal rhyming that this.*

The cataract strong then plunges along;
Striking and raging as if a war waging
Its caverns and rocks among;
Rising and leaping, sinking and creeping,
Swelling and sweeping, showering and springing,
Flying and flinging, writhing and wringing,
Eddying and whisking, spouting and frisking,
Turning and twisting, around and around
With endless rebound: smiting and fighting
A sight to delight in, confounding, astounding,
Dizzying and deafening the ear with its sound:
Collecting, projecting, receding and speeding,
And shocking and rocking and darting and parting,
And threading and spreading and whizzing and hissing,
And dripping and skipping and hitting and splitting,
And shining and twining and rattling and battling,
And shaking and quaking, and pouring and roaring,
And moaning and groaning:
And glittering and frittering, and gathering and feathering,
And whitening and brightening, and quivering and shivering,
And flurrying and scurrying, and thundering and floundering;
Delaying and straying and playing and spraying,
Advancing and prancing and glancing and dancing,
Recoiling, turmoiling and toiling and boiling,
And flapping and rapping and clapping and slapping,
And curling and whirling and purling and twirling,
And thumping and bumping and jumping,
And dashing and flashing and splashing and clashing,
And so never ending, but always descending,
Sounds and motions for ever and ever are blending
All at once and all o'er, with a mighty uproar;
And this way, the water comes down at Lodore.

## A Bird Came Down the Walk by **Emily Dickinson**

*Although only seven of Emily Dickinson's poems were published in her lifetime, she came to be the most well-known female American poet of the nineteenth century and has remained popular ever since and a strong influence on poetry throughout the twentieth century.*

A bird came down the walk:
He did not know I saw;
He bit an angle-worm in halves
And ate the fellow, raw.

And then he drank a dew
From a convenient grass,
And then hopped sidewise to the wall
To let a beetle pass.

He glanced with rapid eyes
That hurried all abroad, -
They looked like frightened beads, I thought
He stirred his velvet head

Like one in danger; cautious,
I offered him a crumb,
And he unrolled his feathers
And rowed him softer home

Than oars divide the ocean,
Too silver for a seam,
Or butterflies, off banks of noon,
Leap, plashless, as they swim.


## The Goat Paths by **James Stephens**

The crooked paths go every way
    Upon the hill – they wind about
    Through the heather in and out
Of the quiet sunniness.
And there the goats, day after day,
    Stray in the sunny quietness,
Cropping here and cropping there,
    As they pause and turn and pass,
Now a bit of heather spray,
    Now a mouthful of the grass.

## The Snare by James Stephens

I hear a sudden cry of pain!
    There is a rabbit in a snare:
Now I hear the cry again,
    But I cannot tell from where.

But I cannot tell from where
    He is calling out for aid;
Crying on the frightened air,
    Making everything afraid.

Making everything afraid,
    Wrinkling up his little face,
As he cries again for aid;
    And I cannot find the place!

And I cannot find the place
    Where his paw is in the snare;
Little one! Oh, little one!
    I am searching everywhere.

## The Mystic Blue by D. H. Lawrence

Out of the darkness, fretted sometimes in its sleeping,
Jets of sparks in fountains of blue come leaping
To sight, revealing a secret, numberless secrets keeping.

Sometimes the darkness trapped within a wheel
Runs into speed like a dream, the blue of the steel
Showing the rocking darkness now a-reel.

And out of the invisible, streams of bright blue drops
Rain from the showery heavens, and bright blue crops
Surge from the under-dark to their ladder-tops.

And all the manifold blue and joyous eyes,
The rainbow arching over in the skies,
New sparks of wonder opening in surprise.

All these pure things come foam and spray of the sea
Of Darkness abundant, which shaken mysteriously,
Breaks into dazzle of living, as dolphins leap from the sea
Of midnight and shake it to fire, till the flame of the shadow we see.

## Limericks

There was an old man who said, 'Hush!
I perceive a young bird in this bush.'
    When they said, 'Is it small?'
    He replied, 'Not at all!
It is four times as big as the bush.'

**Edward Lear**

There was an Old Lady whose folly
Induced her to sit in a holly:
    Whereupon by a thorn
    Her dress being torn,
She quickly became melancholy.

**Edward Lear**

There was an old person of Fratton
Who would go to church with his hat on.
    'If I wake up,' he said
    'With my hat on my head,
I shall know that it hasn't been sat on.'

**Anon**

There was an Old Man with a beard,
Who said, 'It is just as I feared!
    Two Owls and a Hen,
    Four Larks and a Wren
Have all built their nests in my beard!'

**Edward Lear**

There was an old looney of Lyme,
Whose candour was simply sublime:
    When they asked, 'Are you there?'
    'Yes,' he said, 'but take care,
For I'm never "all there" at a time.

**Anon**

There was an old lady of Ryde
Who ate some green apples, and died.
The apples fermented
Inside the lamented
And made cider inside her inside.

**Anon**

There was a young man of Montrose
Who had pockets in none of his clothes.
    When asked by his lass
    Where he carried his brass
He said, 'Darling, I pay through the nose.'

**Arnold Bennett**

## Reflections

### Leisure by William Henry Davies

What is this life, if, full of care,
We have no time to stand and stare?

No time to stand beneath the boughs
And stare as long as sheep or cows:

No time to see, when woods we pass,
Where squirrels hide their nuts in grass:

No time to see, in broad daylight,
Streams full of stars, like skies at night:

No time to turn at Beauty's glance,
And watch her feet, how they can dance:

No time to wait till her mouth can
Enrich that smile her eyes began?

A poor life this if, full of care,
We have no time to stand and stare.


### Ozymandias by P. B. Shelley

I met a traveller from an antique land
Who said: Two vast and trunkless legs of stone
Stand in the desert.....Near them, on the sand,
Half sunk, a shattered visage lies, whose frown,
And wrinkled lip, and sneer of cold command,
Tell that its sculptor well those passions read
Which yet survive, stamped on these lifeless things,
The hand that mocked them, and the heart that fed:
And on the pedestal these words appear:
'My name is Ozymandias, king of kings:
Look on my works, ye Mighty, and despair!'
Nothing beside remains.  Round the decay
Of that colossal wreck, boundless and bare
The lone and level sands stretch far away.

## It Rains by Edward Thomas

It rains, and nothing stirs within the fence
Anywhere through the orchard's untrodden, dense
Forest of parsley. The great diamonds
Of rain on the grassblades there is none to break,
Or the fallen petals further down to shake.

And I am nearly as happy as possible
To search the wilderness in vain though well,
To think of two walking, kissing there,
Drenched, yet forgetting the kisses of the rain:
Sad, too, to think that never, never again,

Unless alone, so happy shall I walk
In the rain. When I turn away, on its fine stalk
Twilight has fined to naught, the parsley flower
Figures, suspended still and ghostly white,
The past hovering as it revisits the light.

## Humming-Bird by D. H. Lawrence

I can imagine, in some otherworld
Primeval-dumb, far back
In that most awful stillness, that only gasped and hummed,
Humming-birds raced down the avenues.

Before anything had a soul,
While life was a heave of Matter, half inanimate,
This little bit chipped off in brilliance
And went whizzing through the slow, vast, succulent stems.

I believe there were no flowers then,
In the world where the humming-bird flashed ahead of creation.
I believe he pierced the slow vegetable veins with his long beak.

Probably he was big
As mosses, and little lizards, they say, were once big.
Probably he was a jabbing, terrifying monster.

We look at him through the wrong end of the long telescope of Time.
Luckily for us.

## On His Blindness by John Milton

When I consider how my light is spent,
    E're half my days, in this dark world and wide,
    And that one Talent which is death to hide,
Lodg'd with me useless, though my Soul more bent
To serve therewith my Maker, and present
    My true account, least he returning chide,
    Doth God exact day-labour, light deny'd,
I fondly ask; But patience to prevent
    That murmur, soon replies, God doth not need
Either man's work or his own gifts, who best
    Bear his mild yoak, they serve him best, his State
    Is Kingly. Thousands at his bidding speed
And post o're Land and Ocean without rest:
    They also serve who only stand and waite.

## The Seven Ages of Man by William Shakespeare

*(Written not as a poem but as a speech for Jaques, one of the characters in Shakespeare's play 'As You Like It.' In this speech he reflects on the passage of life.)*

All the world's a stage,
And all the men and women merely players:
They have their exits and their entrances;
And one man in his time plays many parts,
His acts being seven ages. At first the infant,
Mewling and puking in the nurse's arms.
And then the whining schoolboy, with his satchel
And shining morning face, creeping like snail
Unwillingly to school. And then the lover,
Sighing like furnace, with a woeful ballad
Made to his mistress' eyebrow. Then a soldier
Full of strange oaths, and bearded like the pard,
Jealous in honour, sudden and quick in quarrel,
Seeking the bubble reputation
Even in the cannon's mouth. And then the justice,
In fair round belly with good capon lin'd,
With eyes severe, and beard of formal cut,
Full of wise saws and modern instances;
And so he plays his part. The sixth age shifts
Into the lean and slipper'd pantaloon,
With spectacles on nose and pouch on side,
His youthful hose well sav'd, a world too wide
For his shrunk shank; and his big manly voice,
Turning again toward childish treble, pipes
And whistles in his sound. Last scene of all,
That ends this strange eventful history,
Is second childishness and mere oblivion,
Sans teeth, sans eyes, sans taste, sans everything.

# WRITING YOUR OWN

*In this section of the book there are a number of poems on a variety of subjects which are intended to act as a kind of inspiration for your own writing. Sometimes it can be quite a useful exercise to imitate the style or structure of the great writers of the past.*

## WRITING EXERCISE 1

**To a Poet a Thousand Years Hence** by **James Elroy Flecker**

> I who am dead a thousand years
> And wrote this sweet archaic song,
> Send you my words for messengers
> The way I shall not pass along.
>
> I care not if you bridge the seas
> Or ride secure the cruel sky,
> Or build consummate palaces
> Of metal or of masonry.
>
> But have you wine and music still,
> And statues and a bright-eyed love,
> And foolish thoughts of good and ill,
> And prayers to them who sit above?
>
> How shall we conquer? Like a wind
> That falls at eve our fancies blow,
> And old Maeonides the blind
> Said it three thousand years ago.
>
> O friend unseen, unborn, unknown,
> Student of our sweet English tongue,
> Read out my words at night, alone:
> I was a poet, I was young.
>
> Since I can never see your face,
> And never shake you by the hand,
> I send my soul through time and space
> To greet you. You will understand.

1   What is meant by the phrase 'consummate palaces'?

2   How would you describe the form and rhyming pattern of this poem?

3   Flecker wrote this poem almost a hundred years ago. He died in 1915 at the early age of thirty and yet he is still speaking to us today through his poetry. Other poets in this book have been dead for much longer than that and their voices are still heard. What would you like to say to someone who might read your words in a hundred years' time? Flecker asks questions, knowing well that he cannot hear the answers. What questions would you ask? Write down your thoughts and, if you can, form them into a short poem.

**Winter** by **John Clare**

> Old January, clad in crispy rime,
> Comes hirpling in and often makes a stand;
> The hasty snowstorm ne'er disturbs his time;
> He needs no pace but beats his dithering hand.
> And February, like a timid maid,
> Smiling and sorrowing follows in his train,
> Huddled in cloak, of mirey roads afraid;
> She hastens on to greet her home again.
> Then March, the prophetess by storms inspired,
> Gazes in rapture on the troubled sky,
> And then in headlong fury, madly fired,
> She bids the hail-storm boil and hurry by.
> Yet 'neath the blackest cloud a sunbeam flings
> Its cheering promise of returning Spring.

1   How many lines does this poem have?

2   How many syllables are there in each line?

3   How many divisions are there in the poem?

4   What are these divisions called?

5   What is the rhyming pattern?

6   What is the overall name for this form of poem?

7   What do you think the word 'hirpling' means?

8   The poem contains one simile. What is it?

9   There are a number of effective metaphors used in this poem. Describe them.

10   Choose the three months of Spring, Summer **or** Winter and make notes on how you would describe those months. You may even like to compose them into a poem following John Clare's pattern.

**Alliterations  (Anon)**

> Ten thousand trippers took twenty-three trains
> To take them to Trincomalee.
> They talked, they tittered then took their tea,
> The tales they told together then!
> The tricks they tried till ten to ten!
> Till tardy time told them the tale
> To take themselves to the townward trail.

- This little seven-lined poem, as well as playing with alliteration of the letter 'T' has a very satisfying rhythm. Write a similar poem but use another consonant.

**A New Song of Similes** by **John Gay**

> Pert as a pear-monger I'd be,
>     If Molly were but kind;
> Cool as a cucumber could see
>     The rest of womankind.
>
> Like a stuck pig I gaping stare,
>     And eye her o'er and o'er;
> Lean as a rake with sighs and care,
>     Sleek as a mouse before.
>
> Plump as a partridge was I known,
>     And soft as silk my skin,
> My cheeks as fat as butter grown;
>     But as a groat now thin!
>
> I, melancholy as a cat,
>     And kept awake to weep;
> But she, insensible of that,
>     Sound as a top can sleep.
>
> Hard is her heart as flint or stone,
>     She laughs to see me pale;
> And merry as a grig is grown,
>     And brisk as bottled ale.
>
> The God of Love at her approach
>     Is busy as a bee;
> Hearts, sound as any bell or roach,
>     Are smit and sigh like me.
>
> Ay me! as thick as hops or hail,
>     The fine men crowd about her;
> But soon as dead as a door nail
>     Shall I be, if without her.

1   There are some words in this poem that may be unfamiliar to you. If so, look them up in a dictionary in order to be able to give the meanings of: pert, pear-monger, groat, grig, smit (short for smitten?)

2   A simile that is over-used may become a cliché.
Make a list of those similes you think have become clichés.

3   Write a short poem of your own that contains a number of effective similes.

## A Birthday by Christina Rossetti

> My heart is like a singing bird
>     Whose nest is in a watered shoot;
> My heart is like an apple tree
>     Whose boughs are bent with thick-set fruit;
> My heart is like a rainbow shell
>     That paddles in a halcyon sea;
> My heart is gladder than all these
>     Because my love is come to me.
>
> Raise me a dais of silk and down
>     Hang it with vair and purple dyes;
> Carve it in doves and pomegranates
>     And peacocks with a hundred eyes;
> Work it in gold and silver grapes,
>     In leaves and silver fleur-de-lis;
> Because the birthday of my life
>     Is come, my love is come to me.

1 There may be a few words you will need to look up in a dictionary. What is meant by: halcyon? dais? vair? fleur de lys?

2 Why is a peacock described as having a hundred eyes?

3 How many similes can you find in the first verse? What are they?

4 What is the rhyming pattern in this poem?

5 Christina Rossetti calls this poem 'A Birthday' but do you think it is really about a birthday? If not, why has she called it that?

6 Imagine something happening that would make you happier than you have ever been before. How would you describe your heart? With what things would you compare it? Write a poem in the same style as Christina Rossetti.

> Gently Spring rain falls.
> All things in my garden grow
> Still more beautiful.
>
> **Kaga no Chiyo**

*Writing haiku can be very satisfying. Remember the form: three lines with a total of seventeen syllables arranged 5 – 7 – 5 and there does not have to be any rhyme. Although the subjects of haiku are frequently to do with Nature they do not **have** to be.*

- Write a haiku that creates an effective picture by using very few words.

**The Glimpse** by **Thomas Hardy**

> She sped through the door
> And, following in haste,
> And stirred to the core,
> I entered hot-faced;
> But I could not find her,
> No sign was behind her.
> 'Where is she?' I said:
> 'Who?' they asked that sat there;
> 'Not a soul's come in sight.'
> 'A maid with red hair.'
> 'Ah.' They paled. 'She is dead.
> People see her at night,
> But you are the first
> On whom she has burst
> In the keen common light.'
>
> It was ages ago,
> When I was quite strong:
> I have waited since, - 0,
> I have waited so long!
> Yea, I set me to own
> The house, where now lone
> I dwell in void rooms
> Booming hollow as tombs!
> But I never come near her,
> Though nightly I hear her.
> And my cheek has grown thin
> And my hair has grown gray
> With this waiting therein;
> But she still keeps away!

- Thomas Hardy has chosen to write this little ghost story in the form of a poem, told in the first person.

  Rewrite it as a short story in the third person **or** write a script for a short film.

### He Wishes for the Cloths of Heaven by W. B. Yeats

> *Had I the heavens' embroidered cloths,*
> *Enwrought with golden and silver light,*
> *The blue and the dim and the dark cloths*
> *Of night and light and the half light,*
> *I would spread the cloths under your feet:*
> *But I, being poor, have only my dreams;*
> *I have spread my dreams under your feet;*
> *Tread softly because you tread on my dreams.*

1  Yeats' poem is full of images.  What do you think that 'heaven's embroidered cloths' are?

2  What do you notice about the structure of the poem?

3  What is slightly different about the rhyming pattern in this poem?

4  If you enjoyed writing haiku in Exercise 6, see if you can turn Yeats' poem into a haiku, by selecting just seventeen syllables.

### Moonlit Apples by John Drinkwater

> *At the top of the house the apples are laid in rows,*
> *And the skylight lets the moonlight in, and those*
> *Apples are deep-sea apples of green.  There goes*
>     *A cloud on the moon in the autumn night.*
>
> *A mouse in the wainscot scratches, and scratches, and then*
> *There is no sound at the top of the house of men*
> *Or mice; and the cloud is blown, and the moon again*
>     *Dapples the apples with deep-sea light.*
>
> *They are lying in rows there, under the gloomy beams;*
> *On the sagging floor; they gather the silver streams*
> *Out of the moon, those moonlit apples of dreams,*
>     *And quiet is the steep stair under.*
>
> *In the corridors under there is nothing but sleep.*
> *And stiller than ever on orchard boughs they keep*
> *Tryst with the moon, and deep is the silence, deep*
>     *On moon-washed apples of wonder.*

• Drinkwater was an expert at taking a simple scene and re-creating it in great detail.
   In this poem he takes us into that attic where the apples are stored and lets us see and hear
   every minute detail.  Have you a favourite place that you could take your reader?
   See if you can follow Drinkwater's rhyming pattern: aaab – cccb –ddde – fffe.

**Home-Sickness** by **Charlotte Bronte**

Of college I am tired; I wish to be at home,
Far from the pompous tutor's voice, and the hated schoolboy's groan.

I wish that I had freedom to walk about at will;
That I no more was troubled by my Greek and slate and quill.

I wish to see my kitten, to hear my ape rejoice,
To listen to my nightingale's or parrot's lovely voice.

And England does not suit me: it's cold and full of snow;
So different from Black Africa's warm, sunny, genial glow.

I'm shivering in the daytime, and shivering all the night:
I'm called poor, startled, withered wretch, and miserable wight!

And oh! I miss my brother, I miss his gentle smile
Which used so many long dark hours of sorrow to beguile.

I miss my dearest mother; I now no longer find
Aught half so mild as she was, - so careful and so kind.

Oh, I have not my father's, my noble father's arms
To guard me from all wickedness, and keep me safe from harms.

I hear his voice no longer; I see no more his eye
Smile on me in my misery: to whom now shall I fly?

*Not all poems are written about happy subjects – in fact many deal with times of
sadness and loss. When Charlotte Bronte ( better remembered for having written
'Jane Eyre' than for her poetry) wrote this poem, she was deeply unhappy, away from
home and suffering from a bad attack of home-sickness.*

- Is there a subject like this that you could write about? Some people find it very satisfying
  to write down their feelings about subjects that they might find it difficult to talk about.
  And remember, you do not have to show it to anyone if you do not want to.

**Adlestrop** by **Edward Thomas**

> Yes, I remember Adlestrop –
> The name, because one afternoon
> Of heat the express-train drew up there
> Unwontedly. It was late June.
>
> The steam hissed. Someone cleared his throat.
> No one left and no one came
> On the bare platform. What I saw
> Was Adlestrop – only the name.
>
> And willows, willow-herb, and grass,
> And meadowsweet, and haycocks dry,
> No whit less still and lonely fair
> Than the high cloudlets in the sky.
>
> And for that minute a blackbird sang
> Close by, and round him, mistier,
> Farther and farther, all the birds
> Of Oxfordshire and Gloucestershire.

- Edward Thomas conjures up a moment frozen in time – a deserted railway station glimpsed from the window of a train. You can do the same, but first you must **look, see, listen** and then **remember**.

**Storm in the Black Forest** by **D. H. Lawrence**

> Now it is almost night, from the bronzy soft sky
> jugful after jugful of pure white liquid fire, bright white,
> tipples over and spills down,
> and is gone,
> and gold-bronze flutters bent through the thick upper air.
> And as the electric liquid pours out, sometimes
> a still brighter white snake wriggles among it, spilled
> and tumbling wriggling down the sky:
> and then the heavens cackle with uncouth sounds.
>
> And the rain won't come, the rain refuses to come!
>
> This is the electricity that man is supposed to have mastered,
> chained, subjugated to his use!
> Supposed to!

- D.H.Lawrence describes a storm, using vivid imagery. He goes into much detail about the colours of the storm and although he is clearly talking about lightning and thunder he does so without using the words. Choose an element of the weather to write a poem about.

**If** by **Rudyard Kipling**

> *If you can keep your head when all about you*
> *Are losing theirs and blaming it on you,*
> *If you can trust yourself when all men doubt you,*
> *But make allowance for their doubting too;*
> *If you can wait and not be tired by waiting,*
> *Or being lied about, don't deal in lies,*
> *Or being hated don't give way to hating,*
> *And yet don't look too good, nor talk too wise:*
>
> *If you can dream – and not make dreams your master;*
> *If you can think – and not make thoughts your aim,*
> *If you can meet with Triumph and Disaster*
> *And treat those two imposters just the same;*
> *If you can bear to hear the truth you've spoken*
> *Twisted by knaves to make a trap for fools,*
> *Or watch the things you gave your life to, broken,*
> *And stoop and build 'em with worn-out tools:*
>
> *If you can make one heap of all your winnings*
> *And risk it on one turn of pitch-and-toss,*
> *And lose, and start again at your beginnings*
> *And never breathe a word about your loss;*
> *If you can force your heart and nerve and sinew*
> *To serve your turn long after they are gone,*
> *And so hold on when there is nothing in you*
> *Except the will which says to them: "Hold on!"*
>
> *If you can talk with crowds and keep your virtue,*
> *Or walk with kings – nor lose the common touch,*
> *If neither foes nor loving friends can hurt you,*
> *If all men count with you, but none too much;*
> *If you can fill the unforgiving minute*
> *With sixty seconds' worth of distance run,*
> *Yours is the Earth and everything that's in it,*
> *And – which is more – you'll be a man, my son!*

1   In an age of equal opportunities the final line of Kipling's poem may be considered offensive, but when we remember the age in which he was writing, I think perhaps he can be excused. Whatever you think, it is interesting to note that in a recent poll throughout Britain this poem was voted as the Number One Favourite of the Nation.

2   This is quite a difficult task: to write a parody of the poem – still called 'If' but working towards a final line of: "And – which is more – you'll be a woman!" Before undertaking this task remind yourself what a parody is and read again the two poems 'An Old Man's Comforts' by Robert Southey and 'You Are Old, Father William' by Lewis Carroll on pages 38 and 39.

*On the following pages there are a number of poems about animals – always a popular subject. Look at the very different ways that the poets have treated the subject and then answer the questions that follow.*

**Two Performing Elephants** by **D. H. Lawrence**

> He stands with his forefeet on the drum
> and the other, the old one, the pallid hoary female
> must creep her great bulk beneath the bridge of him.
>
> On her knees, in utmost caution
> all agog, and curling up her trunk
> she edges through without upsetting him.
> Triumph! the ancient, pig-tailed monster!
>
> When her trick is to climb over him
> with what shadow-like slow carefulness
> she skims him, sensitive
> as shadows from the ages gone and perished
> in touching him, and planting her round feet.
>
> While the wispy, modern children, half afraid
> watch silent. The looming of the hoary, far-gone ages
> is too much for them.

**The Donkey** by **G. K. Chesterton**

> When fishes flew and forests walked
>     And figs grew upon thorn,
> Some moment when the moon was blood
>     Then surely I was born;
>
> With monstrous head and sickening cry
>     And ears like errant wings,
> The devil's walking parody
>     Of all four-footed things.
>
> The tattered outlaw of the earth,
>     Of ancient crooked will;
> Starve, scourge, deride me: I am dumb,
>     I keep my secret still.
>
> Fools! For I also had my hour;
>     One far fierce hour and sweet:
> There was a shout about my ears,
>     And palms before my feet.

**Upon the Snail** by **John Bunyan**

> She goes but softly, but she goeth sure,
> > She stumbles not as stronger creatures do;
> Her journey's shorter, so she may endure
> > Better than they which do much further go.
>
> She makes no noise, but stilly seizeth on
> > The flower or herb appointed for her food,
> The which she quietly doth feed upon,
> > While others range and gare but find no good.
>
> And though she doth but very softly go,
> > However 'tis not fast, nor slow, but sure;
> And certainly they that do travel so,
> > The prize they do aim at, they do procure.

**The Grey Squirrel** by **Humbert Wolfe**

> Like a small grey
> coffee pot,
> sits the squirrel.
> He is not
>
> all he should be,
> kills by dozens
> trees, and eats
> his red-brown cousins.
>
> The keeper on the
> other hand,
> who shot him, is
> a Christian, and
>
> loves his enemies.
> Which shows
> the squirrel was not
> one of those.

**The Eagle** by **Alfred, Lord Tennyson**

> He clasps the crag with hookéd hands:
> Close to the sun in lonely lands,
> Ringed with the azure world, he stands.
>
> The wrinkled sea beneath him crawls;
> He watches from his mountain walls,
> And like a thunderbolt he falls.

## From 'Auguries of Innocence' by **William Blake**

*A Robin Redbreast in a cage*
*Puts all Heaven in a rage.*

*A Dove house filled with Dove and Pigeons*
*Shudders hell though all its regions.*

*A Dog starved at his master's gate*
*Predicts the ruin of the state.*

*A Horse misused upon the road*
*Calls to Heaven for human blood.*

*Each outcry of the hunted Hare*
*A fibre from the brain does tear.*

*A Skylark wounded in the wing,*
*A cherubin does cease to sing.*

*The Game Cock clipped and armed for fight*
*Does the rising sun affright.*

*Every Wolf's and Lion's howl*
*Raises from hell a human soul.*

*The wild Deer wand'ring here and there*
*Keeps the human soul from care.*

*The Lamb misused breeds public strife*
*And yet forgives the butcher's knife.*

*The Bat that flits at close of eve*
*Has left the brain that won't believe.*

*The Owl that calls upon the night*
*Speaks the unbeliever's fright.*

*He who shall hurt the little Wren*
*Shall never be beloved by men.*

*The wanton boy that kills the Fly*
*Shall feel the Spider's enmity.*

*The Caterpillar on the leaf*
*Repeats to thee thy mother's grief.*

*Kill not the Moth nor Butterfly*
*For the Last Judgement draweth nigh.*

## A Melancholy Lay by Marjorie Fleming, age 8

Three turkeys fair their last have breathed,
And now this world for ever leaved,
Their Father and their Mother too,
Will sigh and weep as well as you,
Mourning for their offspring fair,
Whom they did nurse with tender care.
Indeed the rats their bones have crunch'd,
To eternity are they launched;
Their graceful form and pretty eyes
Their fellow fowls did not despise,
A direful death indeed they had,
That would put any parent mad,
But she was more than usual calm
She did not give a single dam.
Here ends this melancholy lay:
Farewell poor Turkeys I must say.


## Bags of Meat by Thomas Hardy

'Here's a fine bag of meat,'
Said the master-auctioneer,
As the timid, quivering steer,
Starting a couple of feet
At the prod of a drover's stick,
And trotting lightly and quick,
A ticket stuck on his rump,
Enters with a bewildered jump.

'Where he's lived lately, friends,
I'd live till lifetime ends:
They've a whole life everyday
Down there in the Vale, have they!
He'd be worth the money to kill
And give away Christmas for good-will.'

'Now here's a heifer – worth more
Than bid, were she bone-poor;
Yet she's round as a barrel of beer';
'She's a plum,' said the second auctioneer.

'Now this young bull – for thirty pound?
Worth that to manure your ground!'
'Or to stand,' chimed the second one,
'And have his picter done!'

The beast was rapped on the horns and snout
 To make him turn about.
'Well,' cried a buyer, 'another crown –
Since I've dragged here from Taunton Town!'

 'That calf, she sucked three cows,
 Which is not matched for bouse
 In the nurseries of high life
By the first-born of a nobleman's wife!'
The stick falls, meaning, 'A true tale's told,'
On the buttock of the creature sold,
 And the buyer leans over and snips
His mark on one of the animal's hips.

 Each beast, when driven in,
Looks round at the ring of bidders there
With a much-amazed reproachful stare,
 As at unnatural kin,
For bringing him to a sinister scene
So strange, unhomelike, hungry, mean;
 A butcher, to kill out of hand,
 And a farmer, to keep on the land;
One can fancy a tear runs down his face
When the butcher wins, and he's driven from the place.

1 What message do you think D. H. Lawrence is trying to express in his poem, 'Two Performing Elephants'?
 What do you notice about the verse form he uses?

2 'The Donkey' is a different kind of poem. Who is supposed to be speaking?
 What is the allusion in the last verse?

3 What do you notice about the rhyming pattern in 'The Snail'?
 How effective do you think this piece of quiet observation is?

4 'The Grey Squirrell' is another unusual form of verse. Is there a rhyming pattern? What is Humbert Wolfe saying about the keeper?

5 Why do you think Tennyson's poem 'The Eagle' is so short?

6 'Auguries of Innocence' is a fine example of what verse form?

7 Marjorie Fleming was only eight when she wrote 'A Melancholy Lay'. Do you think she was being entirely serious? How old was Marjorie when she died? (see page 66)

8 Thomas Hardy is making quite a statement in 'Bags of Meat.'
 Is his message as relevant today as it was when he wrote the poem all those years ago?

9 Which of the eight poems in this section would be your favourite? Why?
 Use it as an inspiration to write an 'animal poem' yourself.

**Epitaph on a Hare** by **William Cowper**

*This poem is also about an animal – a hare that the author kept as a pet together with his cat – but as you can see from the title, this poem is written as an epitaph after the hare had died. Read the poem and then answer the questions that follow.*

Here lies, whom hound did ne'er pursue,
　　Nor swifter greyhound follow,
Whose foot ne'er tainted morning dew,
　　Nor ear heard huntsman's hallo',

Old Tiney, surliest of his kind,
　　Who, nursed with tender care,
And to domestic bounds confined,
　　Was still a wild Jack-hare.

Though duly from my hand he took
　　His pittance every night,
He did it with a jealous look,
　　And, when he could, would bite.

His diet was of wheaten bread,
　　And milk, and oats, and straw,
Thistles, or lettuces instead,
　　With sand to scour his maw.

On twigs of hawthorn he regaled,
　　On pippins' russet* peel;　　　　　　　　　　*apple
And, when his juicy salads failed,
　　Sliced carrot pleased him well.

A turkey carpet was his lawn,
　　Whereon he loved to bound,
To skip and gambol like a fawn,
　　And swing his rump around.

His frisking was at evening hours,
　　For then he lost his fear;
But most before approaching showers,
　　Or when a storm drew near.

Eight years and five round-rolling moons
　　He thus saw steal away,
Dozing out all his idle noons,
　　And every night at play.

I kept him for his humour's sake,
    For he would oft beguile
My heart of thoughts that made it ache,
    And force me to a smile.

But now, beneath this walnut shade
    He finds his long last home,
And waits in snug concealment laid,
    Till gentler Puss shall come.

He, still more aged, feels the shocks
    From which no care can save,
And, partner once of Tiney's box,
    Must soon partake his grave.

1   What rhyming pattern does Cowper (pronounced Cooper) use throughout this poem?

2   What do you think he means by the phrase 'five round-rolling moons' in the eighth verse?

3   Tiney  sounds as if he is quite a vicious, surly animal at times.
    Why does Cowper say that he kept him?

4   How did the hare get on with the cat?

5   Epitaphs can sometimes be quite amusing.  (see the three on page 18).
    Imagine that you had kept a rather unusual animal and write an epitaph for it.


## WRITING EXERCISE 16

**Two Limericks** by **Lewis Carroll**

There was a young man of Oporta
Who daily got shorter and shorter,
    The reason he said
    Was the hod on his head,
Which was filled with the heaviest mortar.

His sister named Lucy O'Finner,
Grew constantly thinner and thinner,
    The reason was plain,
    She slept out in the rain,
And was never allowed any dinner.

- There are some more limericks on Page 49.
  Remember the form of a limerick – five lines with a rhyming pattern aabba and stresses of
  3-3-2-2-3.
  Now decide on the name of a place and think of some good words to rhyme with it for
  lines 1,2 and 5.  The rest should be fairly simple.

**'Oh who is that young sinner?'** by **A.E.Housman**

Oh who is that young sinner with the handcuffs on his wrists?
And what has he been after that they groan and shake their fists?
And wherefore is he wearing such a conscience-stricken air?
Oh they're taking him to prison for the colour of his hair.

'Tis a shame to human nature, such a head of hair as his;
In the good old time 'twas hanging for the colour that it is;
Though hanging isn't bad enough and flaying would be fair
For the nameless and abominable colour of his hair.

Oh a deal of pains he's taken and a pretty price he's paid
To hide his poll or dye it of a mentionable shade;
But they've pulled the beggar's hat off for the world to see and stare,
And they're haling him to justice for the colour of his hair.

Now 'tis oakum for his fingers and the treadmilll for his feet
And the quarry-gang on Portland in the cold and in the heat,
And between his spells of labour in the time he has to spare
He can curse the God that made him for the colour of his hair.

1   The subject of a poem is not always what it seems at first reading.  On the surface this
    might seem rather absurd, that someone could be condemned for the colour of his hair;
    but stranger things have happened in our history.  It might help your understanding to
    know that Housman wrote this poem in 1936.
    What was happening in Nazi Germany at that time?

2   Is there something that you feel strongly about?
    Try putting your feelings into verse using the same technique that Housman has used.

# POEMS TO COMPARE

## POEMS TO COMPARE: 1

*Two poems, on a similar subject: Snow.*

### London Snow by Robert Bridges

When men were all asleep the snow came flying,
    In large white flakes falling on the city brown,
Stealthily and perpetually settling and loosely lying,
    Hushing the latest traffic of the drowsy town;
Deadening, muffling, stifling its murmurs failing;
Lazily and incessantly floating down and down:
    Silently sifting and veiling road, roof and railing;
Hiding difference, making unevenness even,
Into angles and crevices softly drifting and sailing.
    All night it fell, and when full inches seven
It lay in depth of its uncompacted lightness,
The clouds blew off from a high and frosty heaven;
    And all woke early for the unaccustomed brightness
Of the winter dawning, the strange unheavenly glare:
The eye marvelled – marvelled at the dazzling whiteness;
    The ear harkened to the stillness of the solemn air;
No sound of wheel rumbling nor of foot falling,
And the busy morning cries came thin and spare.
    Then boys I heard, as they went to school calling,
They gathered up the crystal manna to freeze
Their tongues with tasting, their hands with snowballing;
    Or rioted in a drift, plunging up to the knees;
Or peering up from under the white-mossed wonder,
'O look at the trees!' they cried, 'O look at the trees!'
    With lessened load a few carts creak and blunder,
Following along the white deserted way,
A country company long dispersed asunder:
    When now already the sun, in pale display
Standing by Paul's high dome, spread forth below
His sparkling beams, and awoke the stir of day.
    For now doors open, and war is waged with the snow;
And trains of sombre men, past tale of number,
Tread long brown paths, as toward their toil they go:
    But even for them awhile no cares encumber
Their minds diverted; the daily word is unspoken,
The daily thoughts of labour and sorrow slumber
At the sight of the beauty that greets them, for the charm they
    have broken.

**Snow in the Suburbs** by **Thomas Hardy**

*Every branch big with it,*
*Bent every twig with it;*
*Every fork like a white web-foot;*
*Every street and pavement mute:*
*Some flakes have lost their way, and grope back upward, when*
*Meeting those meandering down they turn and descend again.*
*The palings are glued together like a wall,*
*And there is no waft of wind with the fleecy fall.*

*A sparrow enters the tree,*
*Whereon immediately*
*A snow-lump thrice his own slight size*
*Descends on him and showers his head and eyes,*
*And overturns him,*
*And near inurns him,*
*And lights on a nether twig, when its brush*
*Stars off a volley of other lodging lumps with a rush.*

*The steps are a blanched slope,*
*Up which, with feeble hope,*
*A black cat comes, wide-eyed and thin;*
*And we take him in.*

*Two poems with the same title, written in the First World War, one by Wilfred Owen, about whom a great deal is known (see pages 35 and 36), and the other by Elinor Jenkins, about whom I have been able to find almost nothing apart from the fact that she is supposed to have died in 1921. [If anyone is able to enlighten me further I would be most grateful;. M.Y.)*

*These poems are deliberately shocking in their content. 'Dulce et decorum est, pro patria mori' is a Latin inscription meaning 'It is sweet and fitting to die for one's country.'*

## Dulce Et Decorum Est by **Wilfred Owen**

Bent double, like old beggars under sacks,
Knock-kneed, coughing like hags, we cursed through sludge,
Till on the haunting flares we turned our backs
And towards our distant rest began to trudge.
Men marched asleep. Many had lost their boots
But limped on, blood-shod. All went lame; all blind;
Drunk with fatigue; deaf even to the hoots
Of tired, out-stripped Five-Nines that dropped behind.

Gas! Gas! Quick, boys! – An ecstasy of fumbling,
Fitting the clumsy helmets just in time;
But someone still was yelling out and stumbling
And flound'ring like a man in fire or lime ....
Dim, through the misty panes and thick green light,
As under a green sea, I saw him drowning.

In all my dreams, before my helpless sight,
He plunges at me, guttering, choking, drowning.

If in some smothering dreams you too could pace
Behind the wagon that we flung him in,
And watch the white eyes writhing in his face,
His hanging face, like a devil's sick of sin;
If you could hear, at every jolt, the blood
Come gargling from the froth-corrupted lungs,
Obscene as cancer, bitter as the cud
Of vile, incurable sores on innocent tongues,
My friend, you would not tell with such high zest
To children ardent for some desperate glory,
The old Lie: Dulce et decorum est
Pro patria mori.

# Dulce Et Decorum? by Elinor Jenkins

We buried of our dead the dearest one –
Said each to other, 'Here then let him lie,
And they may find the place, when all is done,
From the old may tree standing guard near by.'

Strong limbs whereon the wasted life blood dries,
And soft cheeks that a girl might wish her own,
A scholar's brow, o'ershadowing valiant eyes,
Henceforth shall pleasure charnel-worms alone.

For we, that loved him, covered up his face,
And laid him in the sodden earth away,
And left him lying in that lonely place
To rot and moulder with the mouldering clay.

The hawthorn that above his grave head grew
Like an old crone toward the raw earth bowed,
Wept softly over him, the whole night through,
And made him of her tears a glimmering shroud.

.....

Oh Lord of Hosts, no hallowed prayer we bring,
Here for Thy grace is no importuning,
No room for those that will not strive nor cry
When lovingkindness with our dead lies slain:
Give us our fathers' heathen hearts again,
Valour to dare, and fortitude to die.

*Unlike the two previous poems, these poems are intensely patriotic. Until about 1950 the first was sung in Britain by schoolchildren standing around the flag on Empire Day (24th May). Tennyson's poem tends to glorify the deaths of the horsemen who lost their lives in this incident in the Crimean War.*

**Flag of Britain (Anon.)**

Flag of Britain proudly waving
Over many distant seas,
Flag of Britain boldly braving
Blinding fog and adverse breeze.
*We salute thee and we pray*
*Bless, oh God, our land today.*

Flag of Britain wheresoever
Thy bright colours are outspread,
Slavery must cease forever,
Light and freedom reign instead.
*We salute thee and we pray*
*Bless, oh God, our land today.*

Flag of Britain 'mid the nations,
May it ever speak of peace
And proclaim to farthest stations
All unworthy strife must cease.
*We salute thee and we pray*
*Bless, oh God, our land today.*

But if duty sternly need it,
Freely let it be unfurled,
Winds of heaven they may speed it
To each quarter of the world.
*We salute thee and we pray*
*Bless, oh God, our land today.*

Love of it across the waters,
Passing with electric thrill,
Binds our distant sons and daughters
Heart to heart with Britain still.
*We salute it and we pray*
*Bless, oh God, our land today.*

Regions east and west united
All our Empire knit in one
By right loyal hearts depended
Let it wave beneath the sun.
*We salute it and we pray*
*Bless, oh God, our land today.*

from **The Charge of the Light Brigade** by **Alfred, Lord Tennyson**

Half a league, half a league,
Half a league onward,
All in the valley of Death
Rode the six hundred.
'Forward the Light Brigade!
Charge for the guns!' he said:
Into the valley of Death
Rode the six hundred.

'Forward the Light Brigade!'
Was there a man dismay'd?
Not tho' the soldier knew
Someone had blunder'd:
Their's not to make reply,
Their's not to reason why,
Their's but to do and die:
Into the valley of Death
Rode the six hundred.

Cannon to the right of them,
Cannon to the left of them,
Cannon in front of them
Volley'd and thunder'd;
Storm'd at with shot and shell,
Boldly they rode and well,
Into the jaws of Death,
Into the mouth of Hell,
Rode the six hundred.

Flash'd all their sabres bare,
Flash'd as they turn'd in air,
Sabring the gunners there,
Charging an army, while
All the world wonder'd:
Plunged in the battery-smoke
Right thro' the line they broke;
Cossack and Russian
Reel'd from the sabre-stroke
Shatter'd and sunder'd.
Then they rode back, but not,
Not the six hundred.

When can their glory fade?
O the wild charge they made!
All the world wonder'd.
Honour the charge they made!
Honour the Light brigade,
Noble six hundred!

## To Daffodils by Robert Herrick

Fair daffodils, we weep to see
    You haste away so soon;
As yet the early-rising sun
    Has not attain'd his noon.
            Stay, stay
    Until the hasting day
            Has run
    But to the evensong;
And, having prayed together, we
    Will go with you along.

We have short time to stay, as you,
    We have as short a spring;
As quick a growth to meet decay,
    As you, or anything.
            We die
    As your hours do, and dry
            Away
    Like to the summer's rain;
Or as the pearls of morning's dew,
    Ne'er to be found again.

## Daffodils by William Wordsworth

I wander'd lonely as a cloud
    That floats on high o'er vales and hills,
When all at once I saw a crowd,
    A host, of golden daffodils;
Beside the lake, beneath the trees,
Fluttering and dancing in the breeze.

Continuous as the stars that shine
    And twinkle on the Milky Way,
They stretched in never-ending line
    Along the margin of a bay:
Ten thousand saw I at a glance,
Tossing their heads in sprightly dance.

The waves beside them danced, but they
    Out-did the sparkling waves in glee:
A poet could not but be gay,
    In such a jocund company:
I gazed – and gazed – but little thought
What wealth the show to me had brought:

For oft, when on my couch I lie
    In vacant or in pensive mood,
They flash upon that inward eye
    Which is the bliss of solitude;
And then my heart with pleasure fills,
And dances with the daffodils.

*In these two poems there are two very different schoolteachers.*

### The Village Schoolmaster by Oliver Goldsmith

> Beside yon straggling fence that skirts the way,
> With blossomed furze unprofitably gay,
> There in his noisy mansion, skilled to rule,
> The village master taught his little school;
> A man severe he was, and stern to view,
> I knew him well, and every truant knew;
> Well had the boding tremblers learned to trace
> The day's disasters in his morning face;
> Full well they laughed, with counterfeited glee,
> At all his jokes, for many a joke had he:
> Full well the busy whisper, circling round,
> Conveyed the dismal tidings, when he frowned;
> Yet he was kind, or, if severe in aught,
> The love he bore to learning was in fault;
> The village all declared how much he knew;
> 'Twas certain he could write, and cipher too;
> Land he could measure, terms and tides presage,
> And even the story ran that he could gauge.
> In arguing, too, the parson owned his skill,
> For, even though vanquished, he could argue still;
> While words of learned length and thundering sound
> Amazed the gazing rustics ranged around;
> And still they gazed, and still the wonder grew
> That one small head could carry all he knew.

## Last Lesson of the Afternoon by **D. H. Lawrence**

*When will the bell ring, and end this weariness?*
*How long have they tugged the leash, and strained apart,*
*My pack of unruly hounds! I cannot start*
*Them again on a quarry of knowledge they hate to hunt,*
*I can haul them and urge them no more.*

*No longer now can I endure the brunt*
*Of the books that lie out on the desks; a full three-score*
*Of several insults of blotted pages, and scrawl*
*Of slovenly work that they have offered me.*
*I am sick, and what on earth is the good of it all?*
*What good to them or me, I cannot see!*

*So, shall I take*
*My last dear fuel of life to heap on my soul*
*And kindle my will to a flame that shall consume*
*Their dross of indifference; and take the toll*
*Of their insults in punishment? – I will not! –*

*I will not waste my soul and my strength for this.*
*What do I care for all that they do amiss!*
*What is the point of this teaching of mine, and of this*
*Learning of theirs? It all goes down the same abyss.*

*What does it matter to me, if they can write*
*A description of a dog, or if they can't?*
*What is the point? To us both, it is all my aunt!*
*And yet I'm supposed to care, with all my might.*

*I do not, and will not; they won't and they don't; and that's all!*
*I shall keep my strength for myself; they can keep theirs as well.*
*Why should we beat our heads against the wall*
*Of each other?*
*I shall sit and wait for the bell.*

*Two poems on the subject of Autumn.*

## The Burning of the Leaves by Laurence Binyon

Now is the time for the burning of the leaves.
They go to the fire; the nostril pricks with smoke
Wandering slowly into a weeping mist.
Brittle and blotched, ragged and rotten sheaves!
A flame seizes the smouldering ruin and bites
On stubborn stalks that crackle as they resist.

The last hollyhock's fallen tower is dust;
All the spices of June are a bitter reek,
All the extravagant riches spent and mean.
All burns! The reddest rose is a ghost;
Sparks whirl up, to expire in the mist: the wild
Fingers of fire are making corruption clean.

Now is the time for stripping the spirit bare,
Time for the burning of days ended and done,
Idle solace of things that have gone before:
Rootless hopes and fruitless desires are there;
Let them go to the fire, with never a look behind.
The world that was ours is a world that is ours no more.

They will come again, the leaf and the flower, to arise
From squalor of rottenness into the old splendour,
And magical scents to a wondering memory bring;
The same glory, to shine upon different eyes.
Earth cares for her own ruins, naught for ours.
Nothing is certain, only the certain spring.

**To Autumn** by **John Keats**

Season of mists and mellow fruitfulness!
    Close bosom-friend of the maturing sun;
Conspiring with him how to load and bless
    With fruit the vines that round the thatch-eaves run;
To bend with apples the moss'd cottage trees,
    And fill all fruit with ripeness to the core;
    To swell the gourd, and plump the hazel shells
    With a sweet kernel; to set budding more,
And still more, later flowers for the bees,
Until they think warm days will never cease,
    For Summer has o'er-brimmed their clammy cells.

Who hath not seen thee oft amid thy store?
    Sometimes whoever seeks abroad may find
Thee sitting careless on a granary floor,
    Thy hair soft-lifted by the winnowing wind,
Or on a half-reap'd furrow sound asleep,
    Drowsed with the fume of poppies, while thy hook
    Spares the next swath and all its twinèd flowers;
    And sometimes like a gleaner thou dost keep
Steady they laden head across a brook;
Or by a cider-press, with patient look,
    Thou watchest the last oozings hours by hours.

Where are the songs of Spring?  Ay, where are they?
    Think not of them, thou hast thy music too, -
While barrèd clouds bloom the soft-dying day,
    And touch the stubble-plains with rosy hue;
Then in a wailful choir the small gnats mourn
    Among the river sallows, borne aloft
    Or sinking as the light wind lives or dies;
    And full-grown lambs loud bleat from hilly bourn;
Hedge-crickets sing; and now with treble soft
The redbreast whistles from a garden-croft;
    And gathering swallows twitter in the skies.

**Glossary**

*This section of the book lists the various devices that may be used to express ideas effectively in poetry; in each case it will give a definition and, where possible, offer examples of how poets have used the device. When you understand what the device is and how it works it should be easier for you to discuss the content of poetry and will help you to write your own.*

**alexandrine (see hexameter below)**

**allegory:**      a form of story that has two meanings, with the second meaning hidden or partly hidden behind the literal, more obvious first meaning. The most obvious example is to found in John Bunyan's 'The Pilgrim's Progress'. It tells the story of one of the characters called Christian and his journey from his home to the Heavenly City; but what it is really about is the story of any Christian person and his or her journey through life.

**alliteration:**      a device frequently used in poetry where a consonant, usually initial is repeated.
Example: *"Water, water, everywhere, and not a drop to drink"*
*(w – w – w – dr – dr)*

**allusion:**      a passing reference to some person, place, historical event, literary or artistic work, not explained but assumed by the writer to be familiar to the reader. Sadly this is frequently not so and we are either left wondering or flying around our reference books to find out what is meant. For example, if you look at the final verse of G.K.Chesterton's '*The Donkey*' on page 62, there is an allusion to Christ's triumphant entry into Jerusalem on the first Palm Sunday. Perhaps when Chesterton wrote the poem in the early part of the last century most people would have recognised the allusion; that is not necessarily true today.

**ambiguity:**      openness to more than one interpretation. In poetry it is often just a word, as in the last line of Wordsworth's sonnet '*Composed upon Westminster Bridge*' (page 34): *"And all that mighty heart is lying still."* The word *still* could mean *quiet, not moving* or it could mean *even yet.*

**anapest:**      a metrical foot composed of two unstressed syllables followed by a stressed syllable.

**analogy:** a figure of speech, very much like a simile, in that two things are compared. In an analogy there will be clear similarities in certain features or qualities of the two things being compared. Example: *Time and tide wait for no man.* Here *time* and *tide* are being compared and their ongoing, unstoppable qualities are evident.

**anticlimax:** a figure of speech in which there is a sudden change from dramatic, lofty or sublime sentiments to the feeble, trivial or ridiculous. It is frequently used for comic effect.
Example: *Well, you could have knocked me down with a sledgehammer.* Clearly we expect the final word to be *feather* and the introduction of *sledgehammer* is unexpected and, as a result, humorous. *"When I'm good, I'm very, very good; but when I'm bad, I'm better."* (Mae West)

**antithesis:** Like **analogy** (above) where the things being compared bear similarities to each other, in antithesis there is a clear contrast or opposition of ideas, but in successful antithesis there will be a balance of words and ideas that serve to make the figure of speech memorable.
Example:
*"My words fly up, my thoughts remain below"* ( Shakespeare: "Hamlet")
*"More haste, less speed."*
*"Light gains make heavy purses."*

**antonym:** a word opposite in meaning to another word

**aphorism:** a short, witty saying that often contains much truth.
Examples: *"If God did not exist, it would be necessary to invent him."* (Voltaire)
*"All women become like their mothers. That is their tragedy. No man does. That's his."* (Oscar Wilde)

**assonance:** This is something like alliteration but instead of consonants, the vowel sounds are repeated.
Example: *"Down and around and the sound drowned out."*
    *"How now, brown cow?"*
Of course there will always be assonance in rhyme: *flight – white – bright – knight. "The few who truly knew." "The cat sat on the mat."*

**atmosphere:** the mood or feeling of a poem, taken as a whole. Although the setting of a poem often contributes heavily to its atmosphere it is a mistake to leave it there because all manner of other factors such as imagery, rhythm and even character can be of equal importance.

**ballad:** The simplest definition of a ballad is a song that tells a story. Many of the old ballads were handed down orally for generations before they came to be written down. A ballad often tells of some tragic incident in local history or legend. They are usually written in quatrains ( four line verses) with a rhyming pattern of *abcb* or *abab* and with four stresses in lines 1 and 3 with three stresses in lines 2 and 4.                    **See: pages 14 to 18**

**bathos:** This is similar to **anticlimax** (above) but whereas in anticlimax the effect is deliberate, in bathos it is unintentional and something that has set out to be serious ends up being ridiculous. Take care when writing verse that you do not sacrifice too much for the sake of a good rhyme, resulting in bathos.
Example:  *"Beautiful Moon, with thy silvery light,*
*Thou cheerest the Esquimau in the night;*
*For thou lettest him see to harpoon the fish*
*And with them he makes a dainty dish."*
                    (William McGonagall)

**blank verse:** any unrhymed verse may be described as blank verse but a more accurate desciption of the verse form is that it is written in iambic pentameters. Much of Shakespeare's plays is written in blank verse.
                    **See: page 52**

**clerihew:** a humorous poem of four lines with a rhyming pattern *a – a – b – b*. It is about a person whose name forms the first line and is named after its inventor, Edmund Clerihew Bentley.                    **See: page 37**

**cliché:** a phrase or expression that may once have been original and very effective but through over-use it is now regarded as a stereotype, hackneyed or even trite. In writing poetry cliches should be avoided because they will make your work sound unoriginal. Examples:
*"I think you are making a mountain out of a molehill."*
*"He made the supreme sacrifice."* (means he died, usually in battle.)
*"At this moment in time I am speaking to you from the bottom of my heart."*

**climax:** a peak of interest or intensity within a poem. It need not be at the end although it frequently occurs there.

**colloquialism:** a word or phrase – a figurative expression – that is used mostly in everyday speech, especially in conversation. Sometimes it is used in poetry and can be very effective but care needs to be taken because the line between colloquialism and slang is a very fine one

**couplet:**      1:    a stanza consisting of two lines
               2:    a rhyming unit of two lines that is not necessarily a separate stanza
**See 'Leisure' by William Henry Davies on page 50**

**dactyl:**    a metrical foot of one stressed syllable followed by two unstressed syllables

**dialogue:**    conversation between characters.  It often occurs in narrative poems (see '*The Wreck of the Hesperus*' on page 23 or '*The Lion and Albert*' on page 25) but can be used in other types of poem (see '*Bags of Meat*' on page 65)

**dimeter:**    a line of verse composed of two feet

**dirge:**    a funeral chant

**doggerel:**    comic verse, usually irregular in measure

**dramatic irony:**

this occurs in a play when the audience becomes aware of a situation while it remains unknown to the characters, so that the audience may foresee the (often tragic) outcome in such a way that the characters' words and actions take on a greater significance.  Poets frequently use this device, especially in narrative verse, giving the reader insights into matters unknown to the characters.

**dyads (doubles):**

pairs of words that almost always go together
Examples:

| | |
|---|---|
| repetition of the word: | *neck and neck,  better and better* |
| alliterative pairs: | *time and tide,  bright and breezy* |
| opposite pairs: | *this and that,  up and down* |
| repetition of meaning: | *hale and hearty,  rough and tumble* |
| rhyming pairs: | *fair and square,  high and dry* |

**elegy:**    a lament for some person or thing that is dead and gone, written in the form of a lyric poem, with the sentiments expressed in elevated tone and language.      **See: pages 31, 32**

**end-stopped line:**

in verse this is where the sense stops at the end of the line.
Example:

*Colder and louder blew the wind,*
*A gale from the north-east,*
*The snow fell hissing in the brine,*
*And the billows frothed like yeast.*

(from 'The Wreck of the Hesperus' – page 23)

**enjambment:**

the opposite to an end-stopped line – the sense runs on to the next line without a grammatical pause.
Example:

*Sunward I've climbed and joined the tumbling mirth*
*Of sun-split clouds – and done a hundred things*
*You have not dreamed of: wheeled and soared and swung*
*High in the sun-lit silence. Hovering there*
*I've chased the ...*

(from 'High Flight' – page 36)

**epic:**

a long, narrative poem that deals with subjects great significance - heroes of the past and events of national importance. Space does not allow us to include epic poems in this volume because they are invariably extremely long.

Examples include *"The Iliad"* by Homer, about Achilles and Agamemnon and Hector and the Trojan Wars (so often translated into prose that many people do not realise that it was originally a poem); *"Paradise Lost"* originally written in ten books by John Milton, dealing with Adam and Eve and the Fall of Man; "The Dynasts" by Thomas Hardy, based on the Napoleonic Wars. It is construced as an epic - drama in 19 Acts and 130 Scenes but essentially it is a poem and was never intended for the stage; "The Faery Queen" by Edmund Spenser: knights and kings and queens and dragons are among the subjects of this monumental poem.

**epigram:**

a short poem, humorous in nature and dealing with a single subject. It originated as an inscription on monuments in Ancient Greece but soon developed into a literary form that frequently has a sting in its tail.

**See: page 33**

**euphemism:**

when a word or phrase is substituted for one that is thought to be unpleasant or distasteful. For example, instead of saying that someone has died, some say that they have *passed away;* sometimes people refer to the lavatory as *the facilities* or any number of other names.

| | |
|---|---|
| **form:** | the structure of a poem such as in a sonnet which is required to have fourteen lines of ten syllables each and a particular rhyming pattern; or a haiku having three lines of 5, 7 and 5 syllables. |
| **free verse:** | verse that does not conform to any fixed pattern. The length of lines is often irregular and it may or may not use rhyme. A good example appears on page 62 with D. H. Lawrence's '*Two Performing Elephants*'. |
| **haiku:** | a poem of three lines containing a total of seventeen syllables arranged 5 - 7 – 5.  The haiku originated in Japan and the subject matter is frequently to do with Nature.  They can be very simple and hauntingly beautiful word pictures.  The word *haiku* comes from the Japanese *hai* (amusement) + *ku* (verse).  The plural is *haiku*, not *haikus*. **See: page 37** |
| **heptameter:** | a line of verse composed of seven feet |
| **hexameter:** | a line of verse composed of six feet |
| **hyperbole:** | (pronounced *high-per-bo-lee* (overstatement or exaggeration for the sake of effect.  It is not intended to deceive anyone and sometimes is used humorously.<br>Examples: *Please accept ten thousand apologies.*<br>*I shall move heaven and earth to get it for you.*<br>*We went to the play and almost died of boredom.* |
| **iamb:** | a metrical foot composed of an unstressed syllable followed by a stressed syllable |
| **imagery:** | in its simplest sense it is the creation through words of mental pictures.  However poetry appeals to all the senses, not just sight and so it is necessary to look much deeper.  The main tools for the creation of imagery are similes and metaphors and the whole area of what is called *figurative language.* |

**internal rhyme:**

a rhyme that takes place within a line.  Rudyard Kipling uses internal rhymes in some of the lines in his poem '*The Way Through the Woods*".  **See page 43** and see if you can spot the lines where he uses this device. (*Lines 3, 7, 15, 19*)

**irony:** a figure of speech in which one thing is said but the opposite is implied

Example: *Well that will do a lot of good. I must say.* (It will be clear from the way in which the words are said that whatever it is will do no good at all.)

See also **Dramatic Irony** above.

**limerick:** a self-contained poem of five lines, usually humorous. It has a rhyming pattern *aabba* . Lines 1, 2 and 5 usually have three stresses while lines 3 and 4 have two stresses. The limerick first appeared in about 1820 and the most famous writer of limericks was Edward Lear who included them in his *Book of Nonsense* published in 1845. Lear often uses the same rhyming word for lines 1 and 5 or 2 and 5, but nowadays it is thought better to avoid this repetition. **See: page 49**

**litotes:** (pronounced *lie-tot-ease*) the opposite of hyperbole – it is understatement, often achieved by using a negative to convey the opposite meaning.

Examples:

*He is not exactly my best friend.* (meaning: *He is my enemy.*)

*She is not a bad player.* (meaning: *She is a good player.*)

**metaphor:** a figure of speech that, like a simile, conveys an image. While a simile says that something is *like* or *as* something else, a metaphor goes further and what is being talked about actually takes on the qualities of something else. Look at '*High Flight*' on page 36 and you will find a poem filled with imagery, much of it created by liberal use of metaphorical language.

**metonym:** a word or expression that is used in place of another, with which it has a close connection. Examples: people may talk of *The Turf* when referring to horse-racing; *The Crown* may be used when talking about the Monarchy; *the bottle* - for alcoholic drink; *the Bar* for the legal profession.

**metre:** the rhythmic arrangement of syllables in verse dependent on the number and kind of feet in a line.

**monometer:** a line of verse composed of one single foot

**octave:** a stanza containing eight lines

**ode:** a formal, lyric poem, usually addessed to a person or subject, frequently abstract. The ode is always serious, expressed in formal, elevated language and often very long. **See: pages 7, 30**

**onomatopoeia:** words whose sounds suggest their meaning

**oxymoron:** the combination of words that appear to be contradictory (often used for humorous effect)
Examples: *The silence was deafening. It was a bittersweet comedy.*

**parody:** a work that imitates another work by mimicking its style in a humorous or satirical way. **See:** '*The Old Man's Comforts*' by Robert Southy on page 38 and then read '*You Are Old, Father William*' by Lewis Carroll on page 39.

**pastoral:** originally this was a kind of poetry, prose or drama that was about shepherds and shepherdesses and their innocent romances. It has come to refer more broadly to subjects of rural life.

**pentameter:** a line of verse composed of five feet.

**personification:**
a figure of speech in which an inanimate object is given human or animal characteristics or feelings. For example: '*I Remember, I Remember*' (page 42): '*...The little window where the sun came peeping in at morn ...*' or '*Anthem for Doomed Youth*' (page 36) : ... '*Only the monstrous anger of the guns ...*'. The sun is not actually capable of peeping in at windows and guns do not really get angry.

**proverb:** a short, well-known saying that often contains a great deal of wisdom

**pun:** a figure of speech made up of a word or sentence with two meanings, often amusing

**quatrain:** a stanza containing four lines, usually rhymed with a pattern of *abcb* or *abab*. Most ballads are composed in quatrains

**quintet:** *(sometimes called a* **cinquain***)* a stanza containing five lines

**refrain:** a line or lines repeated at intervals, usually at the end of a verse or stanza
Example: '*Flag of Britain*' (page 74)

**repetition:** words or phrases repeated to create a dramatic effect.

**rhetorical question:**

a question to which no answer is required; rather it is used for dramatic effect. Examples: *'Who cares?'* *'Who knows?'*
In poetry it is frequently the kind of question where the speaker implies that the answer is too obvious to require a reply.

**sestet:**

*(also called* **sextet** *or* **sextain***)* a stanza containing six lines

**septet:**

a stanza containing seven lines

**simile:**

a figure of speech in which one thing is compared to another using the word *as* or *like.*     **See '*A New Song of New Similes*, on page 55.**

**sonnet:**

a poem of fourteen lines of equal length – in English ten syllables arranged as an iambic pentameter.  The English sonnet (also sometimes called the Shakespearean sonnet is made up of three quatrains and a rhyming couplet with a rhyming pattern:  *abab cdcd efef gg.*  There are variations of this.
**See Sonnets on pages 34, 35, 36**   and see how many follow the patterns described above.

**stanza:**

a division within a poem, containing one or more lines, separated from other stanzas of similar length and sometimes referred to as a verse within a poem

**tautology:**

the unnecessary repetition of the same thing in different words
Examples:      *They arrived in succession, one after another.*
                        *He died from a fatal injury.*
                        *She was an unmarried spinster.*

**tetrameter:**

a line of verse composed of four feet

**theme:**

the basic idea that emerges from a poem, distinct from the action.
The theme of a poem is often abstract, such as  *love* or *grief, war* or *destiny*.

**trimeter:**

a line of verse composed of three feet.

**triplet:**

(*sometimes referred to as a* **tercet**)  a stanza containing three lines.

**trochee:**

a metrical foot composed of a stressed syllable followed by an unstressed syllable.

# INDEX OF POETS

| Issa, Kobayashi | 1763 – 1827 | 37 |
| Jenkins, Elinor | d.1921 | 73 |
| Keats, John | 1795 – 1821 | 30, 41, 81 |
| Kipling, Rudyard | 1865 – 1936 | 43, 61 |
| Lawrence, D[avid] H[erbert] | 1885 – 1930 | 48, 51, 60, 62, 79 |
| Lear, Edward | 1812 – 1888 | 49, 88 |
| Longfellow, Henry Wadsworth | 1807 – 1882 | 23 |
| McGonnagal, William | 1830 – 1902 | 84 |
| Magee, John Gillespie | 1922 – 1941 | 36 |
| Macaulay, Thomas, Lord | 1800 – 1859 | 29 |
| Milton, John | 1608 – 1674 | 52, 87 |
| O'Shaughnessy, Arthur W. E. | 1844 – 1881 | 7 |
| Owen, Wilfred | 1893 – 1918 | 36, 72 |
| Poe, Edgar Allan | 1811 – 1849 | 29 |
| Pope, Alexander | 1688 – 1744 | 33 |
| Prior, Matthew | 1664 – 1721 | 33 |
| Rossetti, Christina | 1830 – 1894 | 56 |
| Shakespeare, William | 1564 – 1616 | 34, 52 |
| Shelley, Percy Bysshe | 1792 – 1822 | 30, 50 |
| Southey, Robert | 1774 – 1843 | 38, 46 |
| Stephens, James | 1882 – 1950 | 47, 48 |
| Taigi, Tan | 1709 – 1771 | 37 |
| Tennyson, Alfred, Lord | 1809 – 1892 | 19, 32, 63, 75 |
| Thackeray, William Makepeace | 1811 – 1863 | 28 |
| Thomas, Edward | 1878 – 1917 | 51, 61 |
| Voltaire, François | 1694 – 1778 | 85 |
| Whitman, Walt | 1819 – 1892 | 31 |
| Wilde, Oscar | 1854 – 1900 | 44, 85 |
| Wolfe, Charles | 1791 – 1823 | 27 |
| Wolfe, Humbert | 1886 – 1940 | 63 |
| Wordsworth, William | 1770 – 1850 | 34, 77 |
| Yeats, W[illiam] B[utler] | 1865 – 1939 | 43, 58 |

# INDEX OF FIRST LINES

**Index of First Lines**

# CROSSWORD

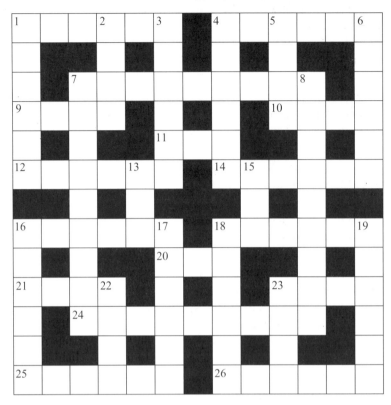

Copy the grid on to squared paper then fill in your answers.

(The completed grid can be found on our website at www.solomon-press.com/PDF_file/poemcw.pdf )

## Clues Across

**1** "And ...... *calling for them from sad shires*" – Wilfred Owen (6)
**4** Moves in a furtive or stealthy way (6)
**7** By author unknown (9)
**9** "*And they wrapped them round that good ship's* ...." - 'Sir Patrick Spens' (4)
**10** Bags of this from Hardy (4)
**11** A short evening (3)
**12** Not liable (6)
**14** Common to Herrick, Browning and Bridges (6)
**16** Yeats' middle name (6)
**18** On a ship (6)
**20** 'Ode to a Grecian ...' Famous poem by Keats (3)
**21** Subject of poems by Hardy and Bridges (4)
**23** The Victorians thought children should be .... and not heard (4)
**24** Spring flowers (9)
**25** Jenkins (6)
**26** First name of the inventor of Clerihews (6)

## Clues Down

**1** Shelley's middle name (6)
**2** Single (4)
**3** Poem of fourteen lines (6)
**4** "*But thy eternal* ...... *shall not fade*" – Shakespeare, Sonnet 18 (6)
**5** "*Not a* .... *was heard*" at the Burial of Sir John Moore (4)
**6** A six-line stanza (6)
**7** Yes, Edward Thomas remembered it. (9)
**8** Shakespeare divided life into this (5-4)
**13** Edgar Allan (3)
**15** A sphere or globe (3)
**16** "*A host of golden daffodils* ...... *the lake*" – Wordsworth (6)
**17** Rhymes with 4 down (6)
**18** Dalmatians C plus (3-3)
**19** What Wordsworth's daffs did in the breeze (6)
**22** "*He who shall hurt the little* ...." – 'Auguries of Innocence'
**23** Emily Dickinson's Bird, "*Too silver for a* ...." (4)